FRUMSPEAK

FRUMSPEAK

The First Dictionary of Yeshivish

Chaim M. Weiser

JASON ARONSON INC.
Northvale, New Jersey
London

This book was set in 10 pt. Times Roman by Alpha Graphics in Pittsfield, New Hampshire.

10 9 8 7 6 5 4 3 2 1

Library of Congress Cataloging-in-Publication Data

Weiser, Chaim M.
    Frumspeak : the first dictionary of Yeshivish / by Chaim M.
Weiser.
       p.   cm.
    ISBN 1-56821-614-9 (alk. paper)
    1. English language—Foreign words and phrases—Yiddish—
Dictionaries. 2. English language—Foreign words and phrases—
Hebrew—Dictionaries. 3. English language—Foreign words and
phrases—Aramaic—Dictionaries. 4. Yiddish language—Influence on
English. 5. Hebrew language—Influence on English. 6. Aramaic
language—Influence on English. 7. Rabbinical seminaries—United
States—Slang. I. Title.
PE1582.Y5W45   1995
437'.947'03—dc20   95-17249
                                            CIP

Manufactured in the United States of America. Jason Aronson Inc. offers books and cassettes. For information and catalog write to Jason Aronson Inc., 230 Livingston Street, Northvale, New Jersey 07647.

בס״ד

In recognition of the סייעתא דשמיא
pervading every endeavor,
I dedicate this book to
my wife,
Tamar,
מנשים באהל תבורך,
who gives meaning to whatever I undertake.

Contents

viii   **Contents**

Acknowledgments

This book has resulted from the contributions of many people, each of whom deserves individual recognition. I hope that, with this insufficient recognition, I am yoitzeh my chiyuv to be makir toiv:

Y. Amsel, Y. Appelbaum, A. Apt, N. Baum, E. Bekkerman, M. Berkowitz, C. Bernath, S. Boehm, N. Bohensky, Y. Braun, D. Brecher, Y. Brisman, Y. Broyde, M. Bulka, M. Cherrick, M. Cohen, A. Danziger, B. Dicker, Y. Diena, A. Dorfman, C. Drebin, A. Dreyfuss, D. Drucker, G. Eichorn, S. Eisen, A. Eisenstein, A. Elias, Y. Epstein, Y. Farkas, Y. Feiler, N. Geretz, Y. Goldberg, M. Goldschmidt, E. Goldstein, Y. Goldstein, M. Gornish, S. Gray, D. Gross, M Gross, M. Grossman, A. Hackerman, Y. Isenberg, Y. Iskowitz, Y. Hess, A. Jakubowicz, C. Kaplan, Y. Katz, D. Keller, M. Kitay, A. Klein, Y. Kohn, A. Kupfer, M. Kupfer, D. Lando, A. Leiser, C. Levine, A. Liss, S. Loketch, A. Lowenthal, D. Mermelstein, Y. Moldaver, N. Moskovics, M. Nadel, Y. Nosenchuk, M. Pam, S. Pashkin, S. Perlman, Y. Pitter, C. Plotnik, Y. Reinman, N. Rokeach, T. Rokowsky, E. Rosenblatt, C. Rubin, A. Schmidt, E. Semah, N. Simcha, S. Singer, Y. Singerman, M. Sinsky, Y. Slatus, Y. Sperka, C. Stefansky, M. Stern, S. Stern, G. Tauber, Y. Tischler, S. Tsirulnikov, Y. Twerski, T. Tyner, B. Wallen, Y. Weinberg, Y. Weinberger, B. Yankelove, Y. Zyskind.

And very special thanks to my good friend Baruch Liefsky for his patience and assistance. Thanks to Rabbi H. M. Levine for his contributions.

The Language of Sanctity:
The Phenomenon of a Jewish Language

The Midrash[1] asserts that the Jews in Egypt engaged in no fewer than four practices that could have ensured their worthiness to be saved from bondage: they practiced no promiscuity; they spoke no spiteful gossip (Heb. "lashon hara"); they used uniquely Jewish names; they spoke a language of their own. One scholar[2] ascribes these four practices to the Jews' distinction in Egypt. That the Jews refrained from both promiscuity and gossip and that they maintained their distinctive names and language meant that they would have been immediately ready for their redemption had they not simultaneously engaged in idolatrous practices (Heb. "avoda zara").

It is curious that the Midrash considers all four of these characteristic practices to be mitzvos. The Torah certainly dictates human activity surrounding promiscuity and gossip. There are, however, ostensibly no specific regulations regarding the use of traditional personal names or of a particular language. Surely, one result of generations of loyalty to tradition has been that Jews, even today, continue to use biblical names for their children. Nonetheless, this practice has undergone a number of changes over time. Names such as Chaim, Ze'ev, and Bruria have joined the ranks of names of biblical origin. Similarly, many names such as Feiga, Reizel, and Leibel have been translated into Yiddish and are used equally with their original Hebrew forms. If there were some imperative for Jews to use only those names found in the Torah, some mention of this mitzva would be expected.

Jews have always educated their children in the holy language of Hashem's communication with His people. Hebrew has, throughout that time, been the language of Jewish correspondence and authorship. However, history indicates that Jews have spoken almost all of the world's languages with greater profi-

---

1. ‏מכילתא (בא, פרשה ה)‏
2. ‏שבלי הלקט: הגדה‏

xi

ciency than that with which they have commanded the language of Scripture. Jews of Spanish origin distinguished themselves from their neighbors with their language just as the Jews of Egypt had done centuries earlier. Parallel to Sefardi Ladino, Ashkenazi Jews clothed their thoughts, dreams, and disappointments in the vestments afforded by their rich Yiddish language. Rashi[3] and others often employed gentile languages to render a Hebrew text more understandable to readers. In no instance is there evidence of the widespread use of Hebrew as a vernacular language in the great communities of the long Jewish Diaspora. Again, it is a cause for wonder that Jews seem historically to have neglected what the Midrash counts among the meritorious practices of the Jews of Egypt.

The same Midrash cites three biblical verses[4] as evidence that the Jews in Egypt never changed their language. Of these, two prove the point by using the word "Hebrew" as an adjective. The third simply reminds the reader that Joseph convinced his brothers of his identity by drawing attention to the fact that he spoke Hebrew, or "Lashon Kodesh." The Ramban[5] intimates that knowledge of this language could not have been sufficient proof of his identity and, by extrapolation, that knowledge of this language could not have been exclusive to Jews. Assuming this to be so, the question regarding the putative imperative to use this language is compounded by the realization that this language may not have been so distinctive as the commentator on the Midrash implies.

Several of the commentaries provide reasons that Lashon Kodesh is so named.[6] Among these, the Ramban suggests that the contextual fact that Hashem chose this language for discourse with His prophets indicates that it is indeed a holy tongue. Expressed otherwise, the language must be holy if it is the vehicle of holy communication. The Rambam,[7] however, posits that the language is intrinsically holy, and he presents as evidence Hebrew's dearth of words for the more inelegant facts of life. Lashon Kodesh, in the Rambam's system, is a pristine language of euphemism and is therefore most suitable to express the loftiest communication.

Common to both these trends is the notion that Lashon Kodesh is especially suited for description and discussion of that which is holy. The term highlights this notion grammatically. While some may translate the phrase offhand as "the

---

3. Rabbi Solomon b. Isaac of Troyes (1040–1105)

4. בראשית יד:יג; שם מה:יב; שמות ה:ג.

5. Nachmanides (c. 1200–1270) commenting on בראשית (מה:יב)

6. The word לשון (Lashon) means "tongue," and קודש (Kodesh) means "holiness."

7. Maimonides (1135–1204)

holy language," closer attention to its structure would result in the more accurate rendering "the language of holiness." Even more to the point, the word "Lashon" itself may convey meanings other than "language." In several talmudic expressions, the word denotes a meaning closer in translation to "terminology" or "diction."[8]

When Isaac, in his blindness, found himself confused by the figure before him, he expressed the inconsistency of hearing the voice of Jacob emanating from the body of Esau with the memorable exclamation, "The voice is Jacob's voice, and the hands are Esau's hands."[9] According to Rashi, Isaac noticed a certain manner of speech more befitting the character of Isaac than of his less supplicatory, more pugnacious twin brother. Certainly both Jacob and Esau spoke the same language with their father, but their respective diction and terminology so differed that to combine the speech of one and the body of the other created for Isaac an inexorably enigmatic hybrid. This "diction of holiness" characterizes those whose chief involvement is with mitzvos. Such people earn the right to be called after the names of their worthy fathers. These are the names and the language that distinguished the Jews in Egypt.

The Satmar Rav[10] claims that it is possible to employ the vocabulary and syntax of Hebrew without speaking Lashon Kodesh.[11] The demands of "the language of sanctity" are different from the demands of learning a second language. When Jews become conversant in the various languages of the Diaspora, they invariably find those languages wanting. A gentile language must necessarily lack a word to convey both the genetic imperative and the inherent obligation of concepts such as Chesed and Tzedakka.[12] If Jews insist upon using such a language for the purposes of learning and Torah discourse, they must reshape it to conform to the demands of "the terminology of holiness." Such does Yiddish differ from German, and does Ladino differ from Spanish.

In America, Judaism has, thankfully, had the opportunity to flourish. Along the way, Jews have principally adopted English as their primary language. Of necessity, however, they have reformed the language to suit their needs more efficaciously. Some lament the prospect that children educated in yeshivos develop proficiency in no specific language, but are able only to string together a few words from several languages. Perhaps so, but the resulting Yeshivish

---

8. Such as like לשון בני אדם and לשון נקיה.
9. (בראשית כז:כב) "הקול קול יעקב והידים ידי עשו"
10. Rabbi Yoel Teitelbaum, זצוק"ל (1885–1979)
11. דברי יואל: פ' ויגש
12. Kindness and Charity (חסד וצדקה)

language is the product of what is healthy about America's Jewry. The purpose of this work is neither to assess the value of the linguistic habits in American yeshivos nor to weigh them against the call for greater proficiency in English. This work merely observes a phenomenon and revels, just a little, in the latest method Jews have found to distinguish themselves as they await an end to this longest Exile.

Yeshivish, the Language:
A Linguistic Determination of Yeshivish

A number of years ago, I received a call from an independent filmmaker. He had been working on a documentary video for public television on the subject of the Talmud. A portion of the material had been filmed in Israel, and an acquaintance of mine had been helping him by writing the subtitles to translate from Hebrew into English. Another section of the film covered a class in an American yeshiva. The filmmaker called me on the advice of my acquaintance to write subtitles for the American footage. I asked him whether the class was in Yiddish. "No," he answered with some hesitation, "It's . . . well, it's English—sort of. Actually, I'm not quite certain what language it is. Why don't you come down and listen to it."

In fact, the teacher/rabbi spoke perfect, fluent Yeshivish. He was never at a loss for words or expressions to articulate with clarity and lucidity all of his deepest insights into the Talmud he was teaching. I then first realized that Yeshivish is truly unintelligible to the uninitiated and that just to translate the terminology specific to the text is insufficient when translating the Yeshivish phrases into plain English. If Yeshivish is not technically a language, it is undoubtedly a culturally based linguistic phenomenon worthy of examination. It was also then that, by writing the subtitles for that nationally broadcast documentary, I gained what I believe to be the only qualifying credential for the translation of Yeshivish.

American yeshiva students and teachers have always used the most convenient available word, regardless of its provenance, to facilitate effective learning. Perhaps inadvertently, they approximate the methods of the Amoraim.[1] The Aramaic of the Talmud is, like Yeshivish, a melange of languages including Western and Eastern Aramaic, Hebrew, Greek, Latin, and whatever other

---

1. Latter writers of the Talmud (3rd to 6th century C.E.)

languages were needed to explain the Torah. Certainly, the goal of ensuring the successful transmission of ageless Torah outweighs any perceived advantage of maintaining the purity and integrity of a particular language. All who have some appreciation for learning recognize that to know what the "Nafka Mina" is overrides any concern about what an English speaker should call it.

The result of this task-oriented amalgam of languages is a mode of speech and communication known as Yeshivish. The casual observer recognizes Yeshivish as English laced with Hebrew, Yiddish, and Aramaic words. Examined a bit more closely, it becomes possible to discern several differences between the English elements of Yeshivish and standard American English. This fact raises the question of whether it is possible to define Yeshivish as a language unto itself or whether it is either a culturally influenced variation of standard English or a technical jargon specifically engineered to serve the needs of the limited, albeit worthy, pursuit of Torah learning.

It is not easy to classify any particular system of communication as a language, or, in linguistic terminology, as a *langue*, which the Swiss linguist Ferdinand de Saussure (1857–1914) defines as a complete and homogeneous grammatical system used and followed by a group or community. This definition is based on the rough assumption that a language grows in a limited geographical area among the people indigenous to it, who are known as a linguistic community. While the definition refers to grammar specifically, *"langue"* presumes a relative homogeneity of pronunciation as well. Yeshivish, on the other hand, is an institutional phenomenon rather than a geographical one. It is heard among people who share a common educational experience regardless of their particular regional accents. It is a language centered almost exclusively on its words and only tangentially connected to its geography and phonology.

Among the only consistent characteristics of languages is that they do not remain consistent. Languages change constantly and universally. It seems that the seeds of language change were planted at the time of the Tower of Babel, or even prior to it,[2] and ever since, the most effective vehicle of communication has simultaneously been the greatest obstacle to communication. The principle of language change is that speakers of a single language radiate geographically and begin to vary their speech habits. The result is that as the linguistic community spreads, communication among the more distant elements grows increasingly more difficult. Another effect of the standard process of language change is that because of the common provenance of the various changed dialects, the *langues* share a common store of original word roots. The ancestors of modern French and Spanish speakers were one nation bound by their use of

---

2. Cf. נח 'פר ,תמימה תורה

Latin. As they moved into different lands, their language changed such that, today, Spanish and French are distinct *langues* related by a shared heritage. Yeshivish again differs from other comparable phenomena in that it is common to speakers in very distant communities and its store of words, or lexicon, draws from sources quite distant from its base language, English.

Linguists examine changes to language at three levels. The first noticeable changes to a language affect its sound, or phonemic, structure. Very shortly after a linguistic community begins to move, various groups develop distinct accents. While England and America differ linguistically principally by accent, only in purely scientific, linguistic literature would it be likely to find the two accents defined as separate *langues*. Ultimately, however, the phonemic system can change severely enough to render comfortable communication impossible among speakers with different accents. Chinese actually comprises a collection of mutually incomprehensible dialects all of which share almost identical grammatical systems. Yeshivish speakers generally pronounce words of non-English origin along whatever American regional phonemic system is comfortable to them. It can therefore be argued that these speakers have adopted the foreign words, that is, the speakers have disassociated them from the parent language and integrated them to the point that they sound like English words although they are not. Only a word using the unvoiced, velar, fricative (i.e., the Hebrew letters ח and כ) deviates from a sound system comfortable for any native speaker of American English.

The second level at which an adopted word changes is noticed at the word's definition, or meaning. This morphemic level controls the types or numbers of notions a word can represent. Discussing this level, linguists call a word the "symbol" and what it represents the "referent." For example, "noise" and "sound" may be responses to the same sensory stimulus, but the choice of one symbol over the other, say, to describe a new variety of music, conveys the speaker's opinion and changes the referent in the mind of a listener who has not yet heard the new music. When an adopted symbol has one referent in the parent language and a different one in the adoptive language, the word is said to have undergone a semantic shift. Each of the new combinations of symbol + referent is considered to be the exclusive property of each *langue*.

English began as an exclusively Germanic language, the lexicon of which stemmed from the same source as those of modern German and Dutch. When England was invaded by Scandinavians more than one thousand years ago, English adopted many Danish symbols and changed their referents to represent ideas and objects more suited to life on the British Isles. The Danish "skirt" was, in Danish, more of a shirt. A few hundred years later, the Norman French conquered England and imported many French words. The English adopted these words and provided their own referents for them. The English symbols "beef" and "veal" have types of meat as referents, while in Norman French the same words refer only to the actual animals that provide the meat. When Yeshivish speakers begin to change the meanings of the words they incorporate from their learning, they are on the road to creating a new language, albeit one limited to a small linguistic community. The preposition "keneged," when used in classical rabbinic literature, has no particularly negative connotation.[3] In confusion with the simple preposition "neged" (נגד, against), Yeshivish adds a negative meaning to the possible referents for this term. Thus, a Yeshivish sentence like "Rebbe's comment was keneged mine" may be translated either as "Rebbe commented on my comment" or as "Rebbe's comment discredited my comment."

The third, syntactical, level is the level at which one language differs unquestionably from another. A nineteenth-century commentator suggests that the seventy languages created at the Tower of Babel differed principally in grammar, or syntax.[4] Yeshivish affects the syntactic level of the words it borrows by its tendency to inflect them according to English grammar rules. For example, the Aramaic phrase "heicha timtza" introduces an explanatory circumstance. In Yeshivish, this circumstance is known as "a heicha timtza," where the phrase apparently functions as a noun and therefore requires an article. Once the grammar of this word has changed to behave as a noun, Yeshivish must provide it with a plural form, in this case "heicha timtzas," a grammatical construction completely impossible in Aramaic. Yeshivish effects such changes to the grammar of all parts of speech as well as to the word order of the same idea expressed in a pure English or a pure Aramaic sentence.

While this particular process of borrowing and integrating words is unique to English-speaking yeshivos, Yeshivish is not the only example of people accepting contributions from multiple linguistic sources to create a powerful tool for communication. Colonialism and expansionism have brought many nations speaking many languages into significant contact with one another. When, for trading or other practical reasons, these people have needed to communicate, they have developed linguistic combinations known as pidgins. The word "pidgin" first appeared in print in 1850, and since then philologists have suggested several theories to explain its etymology. Some claim that it is a corruption of the Portuguese word "pequeno," meaning "small child," because pidgins have simplified vocabularies and grammars similar to those of the lan-

---

3. N.B. "כנגד ד' בנים דברה תורה"

4. הכתב הקבלה (בר' יא:א)

guage of children under two years of age. Another idea is that the word is a Chinese mispronunciation of the English word "business," trade being the principal use of a pidgin. An equally plausible explanation is that the word stems from the Hebrew word "pidyon," connoting the "bartering" for which pidgins have been so useful.

Despite its specific, utilitarian origins, Yeshivish is certainly not a pidgin. Its grammatical structure is no less sophisticated than that of any other language, including standard English. A Creole is a complete language that develops once a pidgin becomes the native language of the children of its developers. These speakers call upon their pidgin to perform all the necessary cognitive and communicative tasks of language, and they quickly add to the pidgin all the standard grammatical and lexical devices of all languages. While Yeshivish, like a Creole, is a complete language, it cannot be classified as a Creole, because it did not arise from a pidgin. To classify as a pidgin or a Creole, Yeshivish would have had to develop from two or more discernible spoken languages. Yeshivish is the result of an infusion of a limited lexicon, not of a complete language, into the vast vocabulary of spoken English. While Yeshivish words may stem from a number of various languages, they do not, independently of English, constitute an actual, spoken language that, upon meeting with English, developed into what could be determined to be a Creole or a pidgin. It would be hard to prove historically that Yeshivish arose to resolve difficulties of communication among exclusive Yiddish speakers and exclusive English speakers.

Neither is it so simple to classify Yeshivish as a technical jargon. Doctors, lawyers, plumbers, and others who practice particular trades invariably use the terminology specific to the circumstances they face in their professional lives. The words and expressions they integrate into their daily conversations are unintelligible to the uninitiated. Their speech habits constitute a jargon. The difference between a jargon and Yeshivish is that lawyers will rarely employ legal terms unless they are discussing the practice of law, whereas students, or "bochrim," in yeshivos may confound exclusive speakers of standard English by speaking Yeshivish even in the course of completely mundane conversations. Terms borrowed from the most esoteric topics of religious literature slip into descriptions of politics, shopping, sports, and whatever else Yeshivish people may discuss as they determine their place within the greater American experience. Even if it is true that Yeshivish people know English equivalents for Yeshivish words, it remains true as well that Yeshivish words replace the most common English ones, and they creep into the majority of utterances. Yeshivish is the preferred mode of communication for its linguistic community regardless of the subject of conversation.

That Yeshivish immigrants to America ultimately melded their lexicon with that of English was a fortuitous development. Those people generally spoke Yiddish, a principally Germanic language related to English. The grammatical structure of these two languages are sufficiently similar to have allowed one to invade the other relatively unobtrusively. As well, English has been a hospitable language since its early days. The Anglo-Saxons of England spoke pure Old English for centuries before the Scandinavians began to invade them throughout the eighth and ninth centuries. Young Anglo-Saxon children must have gazed in wonder at these strong, mysterious Vikings, and they undoubtedly began to imitate Nordic ways. It is not hard to imagine an Anglo-Saxon mother scolding her child for replacing truly English words with corrupt Danish ones. "Say thee not 'known,' 'taken,' or 'ask' if thou meanest 'bavust,' 'farnumen,' or 'freg,'" she may have said. Later, after the Norman Conquest of 1066, when peasant English children began to emulate the ways of the French nobility, whose lives must have seemed so much more desirable than their own, the admonishment may have been, "Speak not of 'separate,' 'direct,' 'figure,' and 'create' when thou thinkest 'bazunder,' 'fier,' 'rechen,' and 'shaf.'"

Parents of Yeshivish children often demand that their sons and daughters replace those same purely English words with the very terms once imported from France and Denmark. In fact, with the addition of Yiddish expressions and terminology, the users of Yeshivish may effect a virtual restoration of English to a more pristine form. By the way, the last sentence contains twenty-six words of which ten stem from French and two from Hebrew. The remaining, "English" words are: in, with, the, of, to, a, of, a, more.

Modern English and Yeshivish are both the result of a blend of standard English with words foreign to it. Here, too, however, there is a significant difference. English adopted Danish and French words because speakers of those languages controlled and subjugated native English speakers. Yeshivish borrows Semitic words because those words call to Yeshivish people from books. It borrows Yiddish words because its speakers respect their forebears. Yeshivish is less the result of linguistic diffusion than of cultural veneration.

Even if Yeshivish is a legitimate language, there remains a question of whether the yeshiva community should raise a generation of children competently conversant in no other language, such as standard English. Yeshivish faces no competition from English for its superiority as a language for learning, but it is less certain that Yeshivish can serve the full range of linguistic and cognitive needs of people who most likely consider themselves to be English speakers although they may employ Yeshivish terms repeatedly as a matter of habit and training.

There are no Yeshivish writers. The lack of Yeshivish literature means that Yeshivish speakers have no classical, masterful formulations to emulate in developing language competence. This fact severely challenges the legitimacy of counting Yeshivish as a viable language.

An even more serious challenge to Yeshivish is that it exists only in the ears of non-Yeshivish listeners who, like the filmmaker, find themselves unable to understand a Yeshivish speaker. Yeshivish speakers are generally convinced that they are speaking English and throwing in just a word or two to foster a sense of cultural unity. The clearest evidence that this perception is strong among Yeshivish speakers is that they employ Yeshivish for purposes of euphemism, that is, couching unpleasant thoughts in soft, innocuous language. Yeshivish speakers may use very graphic, non-English words to describe quite freely intricate, indelicate details of death, biology, and intimacy with no offense to a listener's sensibilities. A symbol is only vulgar if its referent conjures an offensive image in the listener's mind. The use of Yeshivish for euphemism indicates that speakers divorce a non-English symbol from its referent. In the mind of the Yeshivish speaker, Yeshivish remains a foreign language and should therefore not challenge the primacy of English as the language for all purposes other than learning.

To define Yeshivish in standard linguistic terms is difficult. Those who speak it most naturally generally begin as exclusive English speakers, but it seems not to be a jargon. While its speakers have competence in more English words than in Yeshivish ones, Yeshivish words feature in the majority of the sentences they generate in the course of conversation. It seems, therefore, not to be a Creole, although it is a hybrid of several languages. It does not fit comfortably into the categories of marginally similar phenomena of human communication. Like so much of what is truly Jewish, it is unique. In a treatment of Yeshivish, it is important not to speak of a "language" when one is discussing a "shprach."

The Grammar of Yeshivish:
Yeshivish's Grammatical Uniqueness

A mention of the study of grammar usually raises distasteful memories of dry high-school courses and eccentric high-school teachers. These teachers claim to want their students to express their ideas in writing, but they later mark the results in red ink, indicating that the words fail to express the author's intent. Thus, teachers imply that correct grammar is an impediment to clear expression. Students wonder why their manner of expression should require any remedy if they manage to be understood in the course of daily conversation. It seems reasonable that people should be allowed to speak as they please without concern over adherence to arcane, rigid rules.

In fact, there is no communication without the strict employment of shared, if unwritten, rules. A native English speaker may follow a standard English rule and say, "Today's weather is different from yesterday's." The same speaker may convey the same message just as successfully eschewing the accepted rule by more colloquially uttering, "Today's weather is different than yesterday." Nonetheless, the speaker realizes that some underlying sense of order prohibits a statement such as "Weather yesterday today than's different is."

In the language of the rabbis, "dikduk" is the term that most nearly conveys the notion of grammar. Its meaning is "specificity," and it implies that speakers achieve successful communication when the language they use most specifically agrees with the thoughts behind their messages. They must search the list of language rules for those that would best serve their needs. The listener, or reader, is responsible for matching each statement with an identical list of rules in order to retrieve the full message. During normal conversation this process of interpretation occurs naturally and easily, but it is certain that to ensure communication, both the speaker and the listener must share the same set of rules that they must use without radical variation. For communication to be effective, the rules must be both common and consistent.

The grammar of Yeshivish is essentially similar to that of colloquial American English. It does, however, differ in a number of significant ways. Below is a list of the familiar parts of speech, each with a brief explanation of how Yeshivish grammar deviates from English grammar relative to it.

YESHIVISH PARTS OF SPEECH

NOUN: As in English, Yeshivish nouns can be either abstract or concrete. The difference between these two classifications becomes apparent when an article is needed. For example, the concrete noun "telephone" may be expressed "a telephone." There is, however, no comparable form "a happiness," except in limited usage. The same is true of counting and noncounting nouns where "a glass" is possible, but "a water" is not. In all such cases, it occurs occasionally that the same noun may fall into a different classification from language to language. This book recognizes this fact and attempts to provide an English translation that accounts for the potential difference. However, the user is advised to realize that occasionally some interpretation is necessary.

Most Yeshivish nouns create their plural forms by affixing a terminal "s" as in English. When a noun deviates from this rule, we have provided the plural form. Thus, the plural form for "madreiga," for example, would be "madreigas," as we have not indicated a deviation from the standard rule. "Siman," however, has "simunnim" as its plural and is so indicated.

VERB: This work classifies verbs as transitive verbs (v.t.), intransitive verbs (v.i.), and, where applicable, copulae, or linking verbs (l.v.). A quick review of these terms with any high-school grammar text might be helpful. Yeshivish generally conjugates verbs as English does. The past tense and past participle are marked by the terminal -ed, unless the word is etymologically English and has its own forms. The present tense, third person, singular uses a terminal -s, and the present participle uses -ing.

Yeshivish has borrowed a separate classification of verbs from Hebrew through Yiddish. Hebrew verbs have a complicated system of inflection for tense and person that would be hard to carry over into another language. The solution has been to use the verb "to be" as an auxiliary verb and to treat the verb as a participle. For example, "He was machshiv," "They will be moide," and so on. The speaker considers these words to be verbs but uses them as adjectives. The lexicographer has the problem of providing for each word a translation that can both replace the Yeshivish word and render a grammatical English sentence. This work's solution was to create a new part of speech called Predicate Adjective (p.a.) with a parenthetical mark to indicate transitivity, (t) for transitive, (i) for intransitive. If the provided translation is an English adjective, only the original Yeshivish word should be replaced. If, however, the translation is an English verb, the auxiliary "to be" should be removed in favor of the natural English inflection either with or without the auxiliary "to do," as English grammar requires.

The fifth entry for "makpid" classifies the word as p.a.(i) and translates it "careful." As "careful" is an adjective, the provided sentence, "You should be more makpid to keep your room clean," allows for the simple replacement of the original word with the translation. Hence, "You should be more careful to keep your room clean."

The third entry for "mashma" classifies the word as p.a.(t) and translates it with the English infinitive "intimate." The provided sentence is "He was mashma that he is going to the store." To translate this sentence, it is necessary to conjugate the infinitive "intimate" according to the tense of the auxiliary "was," i.e., past tense, and then to remove the auxiliary from the sentence, hence, "He intimated that he is going to the store." The interrogative phrase, "was he mashma," would be translated with the auxiliary "to do," i.e., "did he intimate." As is often the case, discussion of the phenomenon is more complicated than its practice.

ADJECTIVE: As in English, the adjective may precede the noun it modifies or complement the noun through a copula. Thus, it is possible to speak of "a tasty apple" or to proclaim, "The apple is tasty." Many of the adjectives that come to Yeshivish from Yiddish require the suffix -e to precede a noun, but require no affix as a predicate adjective, or noun complement. One therefore speaks of "a geshmake apple" but proclaims, "The apple is geshmak." To indicate that a particular adjective requires this inflection, the word will have a parenthetical "e" tacked on to its end. The word "geshmak" is, therefore, listed twice, once as a noun and once as an adverb. Its meaning as an adjective is listed under "geshmak(e)."

There are, as well, some adjectives that are etymologically past participles and can only complement a noun through a copula. These have a parenthetical note, "p.a. only," following the indication of the part of speech as adjective. As an example, see the entries for "mechuyav." There is a tendency to create standard adjectives from these participles by adding the suffix -dike, but this work includes only those that seem to be in current use.

ADVERB: Of all parts of speech, English allows its adverb the greatest freedom of movement. Both "He goes often" and "He often goes" are grammatical sentences. Yeshivish allows similar options. Occasionally, the placement of the adverb in one language may not fit so snugly in the other language, but the problem for the translator is generally minimal.

PREPOSITION: Prepositions vary considerably among languages, and their use can seem arbitrary. Americans live in a house, at an address, on a street, in a state, of a country. Yeshivish usually borrows a word from another language along with the original preposition, although the English translation of the word may require a different preposition. For example, Yeshivish speaks of "being me'id on," while English speaks of "attesting to." Wherever possible, this work attempts to find an English translation that accounts for the natural environment of the word within a sentence, and notice is taken of the prepositions. Occasionally, the prepositions cause such a problem that they were either included as part of a phrase (see "mashpia on") or simply had to be left to the dictionary user to work out.

There are a few distinctly Yeshivish prepositions, and they are indicated for part of speech as "prep." Some, such as "by," are nonstandard uses of English prepositions. Others, such as "legabei," are borrowed from Hebrew or Yiddish.

Information about grammar can be pretty dry reading to many. It is, however, elemental to understanding and to communication. As with every language, to appreciate fully the uniqueness and richness of Yeshivish requires more than just a knowledge of its vocabulary and grammar. Language is the soul of a nation.[1] It is necessary to live in the language, to think in it, to rejoice in it.

---

1. In קידוש for יו״ט, עמים and לשונות are synonymous.

About This Work:
An Overview of the Method
Used to Compile This Book

The idea for this dictionary began during a high-school English-language class in a large American yeshiva. The students in this yeshiva are representative of natural speakers of Yeshivish. They learn, eat, and sleep in the yeshiva, and their speech patterns have developed within the relative seclusion of their own community.

Once the decision was reached to write a dictionary of Yeshivish, the first necessary step was to collect the words. Each student carried a small notebook for a week or so and assembled a list of all the words representing nonstandard English encountered in the course of normal conversation. All the lists were then compiled into one.

Initially, we spelled all the words according to a consistent phonetic system. That is, we spelled the words as they are pronounced without regard to etymology or commonly used spellings. We found, however, that the words appeared awkward and that the phonetic system defied common assumptions about how a transliteration should look. As a result, we elected instead to spell each word according to its etymology or to how it appears commonly in print. We realize that there is no official, standard orthography for Yeshivish and that individuals may have spelled words differently from how we have spelled them.

A small group of "native" Yeshivish speakers worked on the definition of each word. We worked with the recognition that a word may have several definitions varying according to context. Note the various meanings of the word "for" in the following sentences: "I bought this for a dollar"; "I bought this for a friend"; "I bought this for Shabbos." The first task for each word was to contrive natural contexts serving to determine both the number of definitions it conveys and the part of speech of each definition. The parts of speech are:

noun: n.
transitive verb: vt.

intransitive verb: vi.
copula: l.v.
"transitive" predicate adjective: p.a.(t)
"intransitive" predicate adjective: p.a.(i)
adjective: adj.
adverb: adv.
preposition: prep.
conjunction: conj.
interjection: interj.
article: art.

We traced each word's etymology back to its language of provenance and listed the meaning of the most original source. For example, if we found that a word entered Yeshivish from Yiddish (Yid.), we traced it further to the source from which Yiddish borrowed it, usually either German (HG) or one of the Slavic languages. The purpose of indicating the word's original meaning is to provide a sense of the semantic changes a word undergoes as it serves the needs of different speakers.

Each definition of every word is provided in language as specific and simple as possible. Following the definition is a "synonym," or "translation," for the Yeshivish word when it is used to convey the definition it accompanies. We invested a lot of effort in these synonyms. The job of a translator is daunting, and we spent a good deal of time choosing our words. We attempted to find an English word that could replace a Yeshivish one in any context and render a natural English sentence. We tried to avoid English words that would sound overly technical or pedantic but would nonetheless convey the full intent of the original meaning.

For each distinct definition, we provide a sentence using the word. We have tried to compose sentences in which the word is used in a natural Yeshivish context. Any who learn or who have learned in a yeshiva will be familiar with the situations our sentences describe. Others may find that the sentences offer cultural information about the Yeshivish community. We have tried to write these sentences such that the definition of the word is evident from the context.

Each entry begins with the Yeshivish word in bold-faced type. If it is a Hebrew, Aramaic, or Yiddish word, the original Hebrew letter spelling will appear in parentheses following the bold type. An italicized abbreviation then indicates the part of speech. If more than one definition is provided for the word, each definition is listed with a bold-faced number. The definition is presented in normal type, followed by a colon and the synonym, which is written in all capital letters. The exemplary sentence follows, enclosed in quotation marks.

Within square brackets, the word's etymology follows the last definition. The etymology uses a number of abbreviations to indicate the original language of the word:

Heb.	Hebrew
Aram.	Aramaic
Yid.	Yiddish
HG	German
MHG	Middle High German
Eng.	English
MFr	Middle French
Fr.	French
Slav.	Slavic

If there are any variant forms or usage notes for the word, they are provided after the etymology.

We know that our work is not complete. We expect that the users of our dictionary will find lacunae as well as excesses. But we believe that this work is the first attempt to examine seriously the linguistic vehicle through which our community executes the loftiest of all discourse, that of learning Torah. We hope our work gives you "asach hanaa."

Literary Selections:
Translations from and into Yishivish

If Yeshivish is to take its place among the world's languages, it will undoubtedly develop a literary style all its own. Perhaps the selections that follow will serve as the catalyst toward a Yeshivish literary explosion. We begin with several translations into Yeshivish of famous English works. We then present what may be the first essays actually written purposely in Yeshivish. The last piece is a translation of a Torah work into Yeshivish and then into English using this dictionary. We invite our readers to judge the quality of this writing and to draw their own conclusions about the justifiable uses of Yeshivish.

᳉

ANTONY'S EULOGY FROM SHAKESPEARE'S *JULIUS CAESAR*

Friends, Romans, countrymen, lend me your ears.
I come to bury Caesar, not to praise him.
The evil that men do lives after them,
The good is oft interred with their bones.
So let it be with Caesar. The noble Brutus
Hath told you Caesar was ambitious.
If it were so, it was a grievous fault.
And grievously hath Caesar answered it.
Here, under leave of Brutus and the rest—

For Brutus is an honorable man,
So are they all, all honorable men—
Come I to speak in Caesar's funeral.
He was my friend, faithful and just to me.

Yeshivish Translation

Raboisai, Roman oilam, heimishe chevra, herr zich ain.
I want to pater you from Caesar, not to give him shvach.
Rishus has a shtikl nitzchius,
The velt is keseder moineia your kavod.
By Caesar it's also azoi. The mechubadike Brutus
Tainahed that Caesar had big hasagos.
Oib azoi, it was a big avla.
And Caesar's oinesh was shreklich.
Bi'reshus Brutus and his gantze chevra—
Grahda Brutus is a chashuve guy,
And his whole chabura, the zelba—
I'll say over a hesped for Caesar.
I hold he was my chaver; by me he was a ne'eman and yashrusdik.

༄

THE PLEDGE OF ALLEGIANCE

I pledge allegiance to the flag of the United States of America and to the Republic, for which it stands; one nation, under God, indivisible, with liberty and justice for all.

Yeshivish Translation

I am meshabed myself, bli neder, to hold shtark to the siman of the United States of America and to the medina which is gufa its tachlis; one festa chevra, be'ezras Hashem, echad ve'yuchid, with simcha and erlichkeit for the gantza oilam.

༄

THE GETTYSBURG ADDRESS

Fourscore and seven years ago our fathers brought forth on this continent a new nation, conceived in liberty, and dedicated to the proposition that all men are created equal.

Now we are engaged in a great civil war, testing whether that nation, or any nation so conceived and so dedicated, can long endure. We are met on a great battlefield of that war. We have come to dedicate a portion of that field as a final resting place for those who here gave their lives that that nation might live. It is altogether fitting and proper that we should do this. . . .

The world will little note nor long remember what we say here, but it can never forget what they did here. It is for us the living, rather, to be dedicated here to the unfinished work which they who fought here have thus far so nobly advanced. It is rather for us to be here dedicated to the great task remaining before us—that from these honored dead we take increased devotion to that cause for which they gave the last full measure of their devotion—that we here highly resolve that these dead shall not have died in vain—that this nation, under God, shall have a new birth of freedom—and that government of the people, by the people, for the people, shall not perish from the earth.

Yeshivish Translation

Be'erech a yoivel and a half ago, the meyasdim shtelled avek on this makom a naiya malchus with the kavana that no one should have bailus over their chaver, and on this yesoid that everyone has the zelba zchusim.

We're holding by a geferliche machloikes being machria if this medina, or an andere medina made in the same oifen and with the same machshovos, can have a kiyum. We are all mitztaref on the daled amos where a chalois of that machloikes happened in order to be mechabed the soldiers who dinged zich with each other. We are here to be koiveia chotsh a chelek of that karka as a kever for the bekavodike soldiers who were moiser nefesh and were niftar to give a chiyus to our nation. Yashrus is mechayev us to do this. . . .

Lemaise, hagam the velt won't be goires or machshiv what we speak out here, it's zicher not shayach for them to forget what they tued uf here. We are mechuyav to be meshabed ourselves to the melocha in which these soldiers made a haschala—that vibalt they were moiser nefesh for this eisek, we must be mamash torud in it—that we are mekabel on ourselves to be moisif on their peula so that their maisim should not be a bracha levatulla—that Hashem should give the gantze oilam a naiya bren for cheirus—that a nation that shtams by the oilam, by the oilam, by the oilam, will blaib fest ahd oilam.

HAMLET'S SOLILOQUY

To be, or not to be: that is the question;
Whether 'tis nobler in the mind to suffer
The slings and arrows of outrageous fortune,
Or to take arms against a sea of troubles,
And by opposing end them. To die; to sleep;
No more; and by a sleep to say we end
The heartache and the thousand natural shocks
That flesh is heir to—'tis a consummation
Devoutly to be wish'd. To die; to sleep;
To sleep? Perchance to dream! Ay, there's the rub;
For in that sleep of death what dreams may come
When we have shuffled off this mortal coil,
Must give us pause. There's the respect
That makes calamity of so long life.

Yeshivish Translation *by Shaya Eisen*

You can kleir azoi: to be, or, chalila, fahkert.
Whether it's eppis more chashuv to be soivel yisurim
That shrekliche mazel foders
Or if it's an eitzah to be moiche keneged a velt of tzoris
And al yedei zeh be meakev them; to be niftar; to chap a shluf;
Shoin; and pshat is we end
The agmas nefesh and the thousand natural klops
That gashmius is noite to—'Tis a tachlis
Someone might daven for. To die; to shluf;
To chap a shluf? Efsher to dream! Takeh, that's the stira;
For in that nitzchiyusdike shluf there's a shaila on
The teva of the chaloimos that would come
Once we have become potur from this tzudreita gashmius.
This shafs a chiyuv to be oimed on a chakira.
This sofek is the zach
That makes this kvetshed out life so ee-geshmak.

THREE ORIGINAL SELECTIONS

Essay Be'inyan the Necessity of the Yeshivishe Language
by Mendy Stern

There are four ikar ta'amim why the Yeshivshe oilam speaks davka Yeshivish. The ershte ta'am is altz specificity. Lemushel, the sentence "He grahde went to the store" doesn't have the zelba mashma'us as "He actually went to the store."

There is a lomdishe pshat, too, dehainu that be'etzem the yeshivishe velt would prefer to speak Yiddish like the amolike doiros, but vibalt not all of the haintige oilam knows Yiddish, as a shvache substitute they shtupped a few Yiddishe words into English and shtelled it avek as a bazundere language.

For asach guys, however, the ta'am is more poshut. Roiv Yeshivishe bochrim try to be shtikky, and to have your eigene language that the rest of the velt doesn't chap is a riezige shtik.

Ubber the emese ta'am is gantz anderesh. If the oilam had to speak a normahle English, they would be mechuyav to speak it ke'debui, with all the richtige dikduk. Mimeila, vibalt the oilam doesn't know English properly, they shaffed a naiyer language so they could speak uhn proper grammar and taina that it's a chelek of the new shprach.

א

The Yeshivishe Menoira *by Michoel Y. Nadel*

Efsher the oilam has been noiheg azoi since the amolike European yeshivos. Or, efsher, stam a modernishe bochur was mechadesh it. Dacht zich, we'll never be zicher about the mekor. Al kol panim, there's a bavuste yeshivishe shtik not to chap that you bichlal don't have a menoira until mamash the zman that the oilam starts to light. Every yeshiva has aza bochur.

The eitza is poshut. You run to the garbage and shaf a few soda cans, which have a chezkas hefker. You take them and are mesader them upside down in a line on the table in an oifen you could be medameh to an emese menoira. Lu yetzuyar there's still eppis some soda in the cans, it's not so gefeirlich. Then you go and shnar some oil from one bochur and wicks from another bochur, being very machmir to make a kinyan kedebui. Now just light with tiefe kavana, and—riezig—you have shaffed the most feste, yeshivishe menoira shayach in the velt.

The Yeshivishe Car Buyer's Guide

Model	Ha'aros	Price[1]
Caprice Wagon	Mamash a metzia for a mechanech who comes to the maskana that a van is not shayach yet.	$75–$300
Buick Skylark	For a Kollel guy whose wife needs to get to work.	$200–$900
Chrysler Aries	For an erliche Yid whose wife needs more room for the groceries.	$300–$800
Pontiac 6000	For a tut-zich with some Bar Mitzva money left.	$700–$1,600
Ford Econoline	A mechayeh. The whole family can go together.	$900–$2,000
Grand Marquis	If your shver gets a new one, try to chap the old one.	$8,000–$14,000
Dodge Caravan	Bavust als the most feste van to rent to go to NY for Pesach.	$14,000–$23,000
Crown Victoria	For a chashuve Rav with geshmake Balebatim.	$19,000–$22,000
Bonneville	For a shtikky guy with gelt to spare.	$20,000–$23,000
Mercury Grand Marquis	A riezige makom to keep your carphone.	$19,000–$23,000
Park Avenue	For a shtoltzy lawyer who can't shaf a Lexus because his neighbor has one.	$32,000–$36,000
Lincoln Town Car	The heimishe answer to winning the lottery.	$35,000–$40,000

---

[1]All prices are be'erech and should not be meakev the buyer from trying to handl.

FROM THE INTRODUCTION TO *SEFER CHOFETZ CHAIM*

לבד זה ידוע הוא מה שהובא במדרש רבה פרשת נשא. וזה לשונו: אם יגעת הרבה
הקדוש ברוך הוא מסיר יצר הרע ממך. על כן אמרתי אל לבי. אפשר שעל ידי גם
שהוא מלוקט מכל דברי הראשונים בענין זה ויתבוננו בו. לא ישלוט כל בדבריהם.
וממילא כשימשוך מתחלה את עצמו מעון זה במקצת. בהמשך הזמן שיעיינו בספר הזה
בעון זה הרבה ממנו ההרגל עושה. והבא לטהר מסייעין אותו. כך היצר הרע בעון זה.
ובזכות זה ובא ציון גואל בימינו אמן. ימשוך את ידו ממנו לגמרי. כי

Yeshivish Translation

Zaitik to the bavuste inyan is also what is brought down in the Medrash, and
its loshon is azoi: if you're mamash zeiyar oisek in the chachomim's pshat,
Hashem is mesalek the yetzer hara from you. Mimeila, I had a svara that efsher
vibahlt the velt will be meayen in this sefer, which brings down asach verter
from the chachomim, and will tracht ois what it says, the yetzer hara won't
have aza shrekliche shlita over this aveira. Then, mimeila, if a person is moineia
himself from this aveira just a ki hu zeh, it's a hachana to being meakev himself in gantzen from it, because being noiheg in a certain oifen can shaf even
more gefeirliche aveiras, and if you have a tshuka to shtaig to higher madreigas,
Hashem will be mechazek you, and in this zchus, Moshiach should come, Amen.

English Translation[2]

Peripheral to the known topic is also what is mentioned in the Medrash, and its
diction is like this: if you are really extremely involved in the sages' method,
Hashem removes temptation from you. Therefore, I had a theory that, perhaps,
since the community will browse through this book, which cites a lot of les-
sons from the sages, and will contemplate what it says, the temptation will not
have such terrible control over this sin. Then, automatically, if a person keeps
himself from this sin just an iota, it is a prelude to hindering himself entirely
from it, because behaving in a certain manner can effect even more horrible
sins, and if you have a longing to advance to higher degrees, Hashem will encourage you, and with this virtue, Moshiach should come, Amen.

---

2. Translated in strict, noninterpretive accordance with this dictionary.

FRUMSPEAK

A

ach-dus (אחדות) *n.* Sense of common purpose fostering harmony: UNITY, SOLIDARITY. "The bochrim in a shiur make more progress when they have A." [<Heb. אחד (one)]

ach-ra-i (אחראי) *adj. (p.a. only)* Charged with responsibility: ACCOUNTABLE. "I'm not A. for anyone else's learning; I have to worry about myself." [<Aram. <Heb. אחר (other)]

ach-rai-us (אחריות) *n., pl.* **achraiusen** **1.** Answerability or accountability: RESPONSIBILITY. "Bli neder, I'll learn some Mishnayos, but I can't take A. for anyone else." **2.** Reliability resulting from a sense of responsibility: DEPENDABILITY. "Ask him to prepare the leining; he has the most A." **3.** Obligation, financial or personal, to others: BURDEN. "With all his other A., I wonder how the Rosh Yeshiva finds time to prepare for shiur." [cf. achrai]

a-de-ra-ba (אדרבה) *interj.* **1.** To the counter or opposite effect: TO THE CONTRARY. "No, it's not a good idea to take your brother-in-law as a partner. A. You'll be out of business before you know it." **2.** Polite expression of permission or invitation: BY ALL MEANS, CERTAINLY. "If you want to learn, A., you can sit at my desk." [<Aram. (upon the greater)]

ad kahn (עד כאן) *interj.* **1.** Sufficient for the purpose: ENOUGH. "A. we're not going vaiter today." **2.** Expression used to induce cessation of activity or behavior: KNOCK IT OFF. "A. We could argue about this sugya forever and never agree." [<Aram./Heb. (until here)]

ad k-dei kach (עד כדי כך) *adv.* **1.** Sufficiently to allow: SO MUCH. "He learned halacha A. that even the rebbeim asked his opinion occasionally." *interj.* **2.** Expression of wonder regarding the extent or intensity of something: THAT MUCH. "A?! I never imagined that bochrim could be so mechutzaf." [<Heb. עד (until) + כדי (in order) + כך (thus)]

1

a-gav (אגב) *adv.* **1.** By the way: INCIDENTALLY. "They learned in together in the afternoon, and, A., they decided to meet again later that evening." *prep.* **2.** Subordinate to: ALONG WITH. "I learned Hilchos Shabbos A. the sugyos." [<Aram. (on the back)]

ag-mas ne-fesh (עגמת נפש) *n.* Disappointment or sadness: HEARTACHE. "I had a lot of A. when the Rosh Yeshiva placed me in the lower shiur." [<Heb. עגם (swell) + נפש (soul)]

ain-fal (איינפאהל) *n.* An ingenious, intuitive idea or suggestion: INSPIRATION. "I couldn't figure out how to spend Bein HaZmanim in the country until I had an A. to work in a camp." [<Yid. <HG herein (within) + Fallen (fall)]

ai-zen(e) (אייזען) *adj.* **1.** Well-founded and firm, as in logic: INCONTROVERTIBLE. "He had an A. svara; even the liberal judge found in favor of the landlord." **2.** Perplexing and difficult to answer: UNRESOLVABLE. "I have to admit it; you're kashe on my pshat is A." [<Yid. <HG Eisen (iron)]

a-ki-tzur (א קיצור) *adv.* In summary; in other words: RESTATED. "I tried to find a heter, but, A., no, there's no way we can go during the Three Weeks." [<Heb. קצר (short)] **Var.** bekitzur.

al kol pa-nim (על כל פנים) *adv.* At any rate: NEVERTHELESS. "The yeshiva hasn't collected enough to complete the new building; A. there's enough to get started." [<Heb. (on every facet)]

als (אלס) *prep.* **1.** Because of: DUE TO. "A. what do you feel the Yeshiva is treating him specially?" *conj.* **2.** Due to the fact that: SINCE, BECAUSE. "I wasn't by Shachris A. I overslept." [<Yid. <HG als (as)] **Var.** altz.

al tnai (על תנאי) **Cf.** tnai.

altz *Var. of* als.

a-mol (אמאל) *adv.* **1.** In past times: FORMERLY, ONCE. "A., when I was younger, there weren't so many Yeshivos in America." **2.** With sporadic frequency: OCCASIONALLY, RARELY. "A. he has a chidush, but mostly he just speaks out achroinim." [<Yid. <HG einmal (one time)]

a-mol-i-ke (אמאליקע) *adj.* Foregone, of times past: OLDEN, OBSOLETE. "The A. gemaros used to fall apart because of their cheap bindings." [cf. amol + -ike]

an-shul-diks (אנשולדיקס) *polite expression.* Apology for trivial or unintentional interruption or indiscretion: PARDON. "A. I didn't mean to bother you while you're learning." [<Yid. <HG anschuldigen (accuse)]

a-rain ge-tun (הערײן געטאָן) *adj. (p.a. only)* Completely occupied or involved, as of the mind or attention: ENGROSSED. "He was so A. in his learning that he skipped lunch and dinner." [<Yid. <HG herein (within) + tun (do)]

a-sach (אַ סך) *adj.* Great in amount, degree, or number: A LOT OF. "In the back of his desk, I found A. interesting, old bills that would interest the IRS." [<Yid. אַ (indefinite article) + <Heb. סך (amount)] **Var.** a-zach.

a-ser (אסרן) *vt.* To effect a prohibition upon: PROHIBIT. "The Rosh Yeshivos A. having small appliances in the dorm." [<Yid. <Heb. cf. asur]

a-sur (אסור) *adj. (p.a. only)* Prohibited, especially by authority, from having or doing something: FORBIDDEN. "It's A. for bochrim to smoke while they are in the Yeshiva." [<Heb. אסר (tie)]

a-va-da *Var. of* vada.

av-la (עוולה) *n.* A wrong perpetrated intentionally: INJUSTICE. "It's an A. for a teacher to lower a grade for personal reasons." [<Heb. עול (iniquity)]

a-za (אַזאַ) *adj. & art.* **1.** Being of a particular variety: A KIND OF, A CERTAIN. "The Doctor has A. machine to know your blood pressure even over the phone." **2.** Of considerable intensity: SUCH A(N). "He's A. masmid; he even learns on the bus." [<cf. azoi + Yid. אַ (indefinite article)]

a-zach *Var. of* asach.

a-zoi (אַזױ) *adv.* **1.** With noteworthy intensity: SO. "The shmooze was A. boring; nobody could stay awake." **2.** As indicated: LIKE SO. "If you keep your shiur notes A., you'll be able to find things faster." [<Yid. <HG also (thus)]
— **N.B.** The phrase "azoi un azoi" intensifies the meaning of azoi def. 2 implying: EXACTLY SO.

B

ba-al dik-duk (בעל דקדוק) *Var. of* medakdek, def. 6.

ba-al gai-va (בעל גאוה) **Cf.** gaiva.

ba-al shi-ta (בעל שיטה) **Cf.** shitos.

bahlt (באלד) *adv.* **1.** Without undue lapse of time: SOON. "Run to the dining room, because B. they'll be out of meat." **2.** Almost or practically: JUST ABOUT. "Run to the dining room, because the meat's B. gone." [<Yid. <HG bald (soon)]

bai-lus (בעלות) *n.* Sovereignty or ownership: DOMINION. "My boss constantly creates new rules just to show his B." [<Emulative of Heb. בעל (master)]

ba-kant(e) (בעקאנט) *adj.* **1.** Versed or acquainted, or being so: FAMOUS, FAMILIAR. "That bochur is too B. with baseball stats to be very serious about his learning." [<Yid. <HG kennen (to know)]

ba-ko-sha (בקשה) *n.* An act desired of another person: REQUEST. "He made a B. for everyone to stay quiet while he said his vort." [<Heb. בקש (seek)]

bal-e-bat-ish(e) (בעל-הבתיש) *adj.* **1.** Contemporary with secular style or form: STYLISH. "His new Lincoln is too B. for a guy in Kollel." **2.** Characterized by doing that which is accepted in a specific situation: PROPER. "At least the Chassan was B. enough to remember to go around greeting the guests." **3.** Essentially basic, uncomplicated, and/or undeveloped: ELEMENTARY. "A real talmid chacham would be embarrassed to say such a B. chabura." [<Yid. <Heb. בעל (master) + הבית (the house)]

bal kish-ron (בעל כשרון) *n.* One with the potential to develop further: PRODIGY. "The Rosh Yeshiva had been known as a B. since his early years." [<Heb. בעל (master) + כשר (proper)]

bat-lan (בטלן) *n., pl.* **batlanim** One who consistently wastes time: BUM, FAINÉANT. "They didn't let him stay in the Yeshiva because he was, plain and poshut, a B." [cf. battel]

bat-tel (באטלען) *vt. & vi.* To waste time or to cause to waste time, especially regarding learning: IDLE. "I'm going to change my chavrusa if he doesn't stop trying to B. constantly." [<Yid. <Heb. בטל (null)]
— **N.B.** The transitive verb battel may assume the variant p.a.(t) form "mevattel."

ba-tul-la (בטלה) *n.* Wasted time: OTIOSITY, IDLENESS. "The class clown caused a lot of B. during seder." [cf. battel]

ba-vorn (באווארנען) *vt.* To realize the existence of and to resolve in advance: ANTICIPATE. "The Rebbe B. all the kashes by speaking out the major achroinim from the start." [<Yid. <HG warnen (warn)]

ba-vust(e) (בעוואוסט) *adj.* **1.** Widely known: FAMOUS. "The shiur was boring, just the usual, B. kashes." **2.** Widely recognized: KNOWN. "It's B. that the Earth is round." [<Yid. <HG wissen (know)]

ba-zun-der(e) (בעזונדער) *adj.* **1.** Unrelated or only marginally related: SEPARATE. "Whether to switch yeshivos is a B. question; I just want to finish the zman on good terms." **2.**

Consisting of different or unconnected elements: DISTINCT. "We were meyashev the shverkait by discovering that the sefer attempted to deal with several B. topics at the same time." [<Yid. <HG sondern (separate)]

be-dav-ka (בדווקא) *adv.* After careful consideration; with intention and purpose: DELIBERATELY. "He B. goes to the same run-down bungalow colony just to assure the owner's parnasa." [cf. davka]

be-de-rech klal (בדרך כלל) *adv.* As a general rule: USUALLY. "Unless there is a special shiur, we B. break for lunch at around 1:00." [<Heb. דרך (way) + כלל (include)]

be-di-e-ved (בדיעבד) *adv.* **1.** Under duress, or done when no options are available: AS A LAST RESORT. "If it's too loud in the Beis Medrash, B. you can learn in the Ezras Nashim." **2.** Resentfully; without enthusiasm: BEGRUDGINGLY. "I would prefer not to learn with him, but if I do so, I do it B." **3.** Done just well enough to fulfill a need or duty: PERFUNCTORILY. "It's best to learn Musar every day, but B. once a week is the minimum." *n.* **4.** That which just passes muster, but is not optimal: LAST RESORT. "I know this is not a very Shabbosdik hat, but I took it as a B." [<Aram. (having done)]

be-di-e-ved-ik(e) (בדיעבדיק) *adj.* **1.** Just passing muster: MEDIOCRE.

"It's a B. car, but it'll do for Bein HaZmanim." **2.** Just performing a task according to minimal requirements: EXPEDIENT. "To read straight from the Kitzur Shulchan Aruch is a B. way to learn halacha." [cf. bedieved]

be-doi-chek (בדוחק) *adv.* **1.** With reservations: RELUCTANTLY. "I knew he hadn't listened to me, but I accepted the Mashgiach's decision B." **2.** Only in order to pass muster and to proceed: PERFUNCTORILY, IN A PINCH. "Let's just use his pshat for now and go vaiter in the gemara." [cf. doichek(e)]
—**N.B.** The variant form "bedoichek gadol" is more emphatic.

be-e-mes (באמת) *adv.* **1.** As a matter of fact (implying the subjunctive mood): ACTUALLY. "B. I would go with you, but I have to wait for my brother." **2** Truly or genuinely: REALLY. "There's B. no need for you to take me with you." [cf. emes]
Var. be'emesen.

be-e-mes-en *Var. of* beemes.

be-e-rech (בערך) *adv.* Nearly correct or precise: APPROXIMATELY. "There are B. 1,000 seforim in the Beis Medrash." [<Heb. ערך (arrange)]

be-e-tzem (בעצם) *adv.* **1.** Really or truly: IN FACT. "B. the Mashgiach wasn't looking, but I decided to put the radio away, anyhow." **2.** Being an inherent part of something: INTRIN-

SICALLY. "It wasn't until he went to learn in Eretz Yisroel that he realized that he is B. an American." [cf. etzem]

be-fei-rush (בפירוש) *adv.* Exactly as written, spoken, or intended: EXPLICITLY. "The Rosh Yeshiva said B. that no one can stay in the Beis Medrash past midnight." [<Heb. פרש (interpret)]

be-fei-rush(e) (בפירוש) *adj.* Written, expressed, or clearly intended: EXPLICIT. "There is a B. ban on smoking in the yeshiva." [cf. befeirush]

be-hech-rach (בהכרח) *adv.* **1.** As a logical, inevitable conclusion: NECESSARILY. "A yeshiva doesn't B. have enough dorm space; sometimes there are three and four bochrim to a room." **2.** Proven undeniably: INCONTROVERTIBLY. "You can interpret your father's words as you please, but it was B. a demand that you spend more time learning." [cf. hechrach]

be-i-kar (בעיקר) *adv.* Chiefly or mainly: PRINCIPALLY. "There are B. five common ways to get parking on 13th Ave., but none of them will work unless you're aggressive." [cf. ikar]

bein ha-sdo-rim (בין הסדרים) **Cf.** seder.

be-in-yan (בעניין) *prep.* Regarding the topic of: ABOUT. "I wanted to talk with my B. a shtikl bonus before Pesach." [cf. inyan]

be-is-ser (באיסור) *adv.* By means of or at a time prohibited by law or authority: ILLEGALLY, ILLICITLY. "The boys made a going-away party for their chaver B." [cf. asur]

be-i-yun (בעיון) *adv.* With depth and in detail: INTENSIVELY. "He learned that sugya so B. that it took him most of the zman." [cf. iyun]

be-ka-vod (בכבוד) *adj. & adv.* Suitable, fitting, or appropriate: PROPER, PROPERLY. "It's not B. for the Rav to have to clean up after Shalosh Seudos." [cf. mechabed] **Var.** bekavodik(e), mechubadik(e).

be-ka-vod-ik(e) *Var. of* bekavod.

be-ki-tzur (בקיצור) *adv.* **1.** Briefly or concisely: SUCCINCTLY. "He explained the sugya to me B., but I think I should go back for more details." **2.** *Var. of* akitzur. [cf. akitzur]

be-ki-us (בקיאות) *n.* **1.** Range of personal knowledge: ACQUAINTANCE-SHIP, KEN. "He has enough B. in halacha to be a Mashgiach for Pesach." **2. learn** or **do bekius,** To learn only to gain a general knowledge of a text: SCAN, SKIM. "He learns B. in the morning just to be prepared for shiur." [cf. bukki]

be-kvi-us (בקביעות) *adv.* According to custom or manner: REGULARLY. "He learns the Daf Yomi B. and never misses a day." [cf. koveia]

be-lei-dikt (בעלײדיגט) *adj. (p.a. only)* Having hurt feelings: OFFENDED. "I didn't think he would get so B. by my suggestion that he try a different tie with that suit." [<Yid. <HG beleidigen (insult)]

be-me-tzi-us (במציאות) *adv.* In actuality: IN FACT. "Since he has B. been accepted into the yeshiva, it's irrelevant to question his qualifications." [cf. metzius]

be-noi-gei-a (בנוגע) *prep.* Having an effect upon; relating to: REGARDING. "The bochur argued with his roommate B. the distribution of drawer space." [cf. noigeia]

be-se-der (בסדר) *adj. & adv.* According to satisfactory, acceptable order: ALL RIGHT. "My dorm room isn't great, but it's B." [cf. seder]

be-shi-ta (בשיטה) *adv.* As a matter of belief or conviction: ON PRINCIPLE. "He B. never has more than one cup of coffee during night seder." [cf. shita]

be-shum oi-fen (בשום אופן) *adv.* Under any circumstances: ABSOLUTELY. "My partner is so stubborn, he B. wouldn't agree with me despite my proof that we could save money." [<Aram. שום (name) + cf. oifen] —**N.B.** May presume a negative connotation with the sense: UNEQUIVO-CALLY.

be-so-fek (בספק) *Var. of* mesupak.

bich-lal (בכלל) *adv.* **1.** In any way or respect: AT ALL. "Although he's a weak learner, he's B. not stupid." **2.** To the full extent: ENTIRELY. "He learns all day, and he's B. not interested in sports." [<Heb. כלל (include)]

bif-raht (בפרט) *adv.* Paying special attention to: PARTICULARLY, IN PARTICULAR. "He's a nice guy generally and a good learner B." [cf. praht]

bif-shi-tus (בפשיטות) *Var. of* pashtus, def. 2.

bi-shas mai-se (בשעת מעשה) *adv.* **1.** At the same time: (JUST) THEN. "I went to the yeshiva office and B. picked up my mail." **2.** Occurring at the same time: SIMULTANEOUSLY. "I was able to ride to New York and to learn the Daf Yomi B." [<Heb. שעה (hour) + עשה (act)]

bi-za-yon (בזיון) *n.* **1.** Situation worthy of contempt or scorn: FARCE. "They couldn't even cover the hotel bill with the money they collected at the dinner. The whole event was a B." **2.** That which is not befitting or is beneath the dignity of those involved: DISGRACE. "Their behavior in front of their rebbeim and parents was an absolute B." [cf. mevazeh]

biz-yoi-nos (בזיונות) *n.* Deep feeling of loss of dignity: HUMILIATION. "He suffered such B. when the Rosh Yeshiva found out he had gone to the city during seder." [cf. mevazeh]

blaib (בלייבען) *l.v.* **1.** To be deemed: BECOME. "The knife they used on the ham B. treif." **2.** To continue unchanged: REMAIN. "He tried a lot of different terutzim, but he B. confused." [<Yid. <HG bleiben (stay)]

bo-chur (בחור) *n., pl.* **bochrim 1.** An unmarried male: BACHELOR. "He's still a B. although he's nearly 40." **2.** An unmarried yeshiva student: SCHOOLBOY. "That B. has learned by us for four years." [<Heb. בחר (choose)]

boi ois (אויסבויען) *vt.* To flesh out after initial derivation: DEVELOP, POSIT. "It's a little shaky to B. a whole pshat from just one diyuk." [<Yid. <HG bauen (build) + aus (out)]

boosh out *Var. of* mevayesh.

bo-ra ka-cha-ma (ברה כחמה) *Var. of* borur, def. 2.

bo-ri (ברי) *Var. of* borur, def. 2.

bo-rur (ברור) *adj. (p.a. only)* **1.** Admitting of no question: POSITIVE. "He was B. that his roommate was dipping into his snacks." **2.** Obvious or evident: CLEAR. "It was B. from his waistline that the bochur was not getting enough exercise." [<Heb. ברר (select)] Var. for def. 2. bori, bora kachama.

bra-cha le-va-tul-la (ברכה לבטלה) *n.* A fruitless pursuit or one that is unworthy of devoting time for: WASTE. "I spent a whole day trying unsuccessfully to get my passport so I could go to Eretz Yisroel. The entire experience was a B." [<Heb. ברך (bless) + cf. batulla]

brei-ra (ברירה) *n.* Alternative choice: OPTION. "Since I can't get my passport, I have no B. but to pay someone to do my importing for the season." [cf. borur]

bren (ברענען) *n.* Intensity of emotion: FERVOR. "They learned the Tosfos with a B. in order to finish before the end of seder." [<Yid. <HG brennen (burn)] — N.B. Assumes the indefinite article.

bring down *vt.* **1.** To quote by way of proof, example, or authority: CITE. "He usually B. a lot of rishoinim to support his chidushim." **2.** To discuss in writing or another formal medium: MENTION. "I saw that the sefer B. the same raya that Rebbe spoke out in shiur." [<Eng.]

broi-gez (ברוגז) *adj. (p.a. only)* Angry with or on bad terms with: UPSET, VEXED. "He was B. with that chabura since they wouldn't allow him to join." [<Heb. רגז (anger)]

buk-ki (בקיא) *n.* **1.** One who has special skills or knowledge: EXPERT. "That bochur is a B. at getting into the kitchen after the cook leaves." *adj. (p.a. only)* **2. a bukki,** Being acquainted with particular knowledge: VERSED. "He's a B. in dates of the first editions of all the major seforim." [<Aram. בקא (examine)]

bu-sha (בושה) *n.* **1.** A state of self-conscious distress: EMBARRASSMENT. "The Ba'al Tefila hit a sour note and suffered real B." **2.** A condition of susceptibility to humiliation or disgrace: SHAME. "That guy must have no B. if he can still present a bill after he messed up the order." [cf. mevayesh.]

but-tel (בטל) *adj. (p.a. only)* **1.** Without effect: VOID, CANCELED. "Our chavrusashaft has been B. ever since our fight." **2.** Canceled out: OUTWEIGHED, NEGLIGIBLE. "If there's any meat in the yeshiva's cholnt, it's B. in the grease and salt." [cf. battel]

by *prep.* A preposition commonly used to replace standard English prepositions, as in:
AT "I ate by the Schwartzes on Shabbos."
AMONG "At the Chasuna I sat by the men.
BESIDE "I sat by my wife during the speeches."
WITH "I learned by my Rebbe for five years."
[<Emulative of Yid. <HG bei]

C

cha-bu-ra (חבורה) *n.* **1.** A fairly long, carefully prepared, well-organized speech to a limited group on a particular subject: DISCOURSE. "Although he learned by the same Rebbe as we did, his C. was too hard for us to follow." **2.** A number of people loosely associated by some bond: CIRCLE. "Those guys spend so little time in the Beis Medrash that we call them the 'basketball C.'" [<Heb. חבר (join)] **Var. for def. 2** chevra.

cha-cham (חכם) *n., pl.* **chachomim 1.** One who displays sagacity in Torah knowledge: SAGE. "Every C. deserves kavod." **2.** Any wise, intelligent person: GENIUS. "Even the yeshiva oilam is moide that Einstein was a C." **3.** One who uses his wit impudently: WISEGUY. "That guy is quite a C., getting all those credit cards with no credit history." **4.** One who behaves in a clumsy or poorly considered manner: DUNCE. "That C. ironed his finger instead of his shirt." [<Heb. חכם (wise)] **Var. for def. 1** talmid chacham.

cha-ki-ra (חקירה) *n.* **1.** A topic presented for consideration: PROPOSITION. "The poisek had a C. to treat electricity as fire legabei Hilchos Shabbos." **2.** A treatment of the pros and cons of a subject: TREATISE. "He published a C. on the benefits of involvement in Israeli politics." **3.** An argument or discussion resulting from an examination of many sides: DELIBERATION. "He spent so much time on a C. of whether to take the train or the bus that he missed both and was late for seder." [<Heb. חקר (investigate)]

chal (חל) *adj. (p.a. only)* **1.** Placed under obligation: BINDING. "The yeshiva's policy of locking the dorm at all times was C. on each bochur, who then had to carry a key." **2.** Laid on to be endured, obeyed, or fulfilled: INCUMBENT. "The chiyuv to learn is C. on you as soon as seder starts." **3.** Actually operative or functioning: EFFECTIVE. "The issur melocha on Shabbos is C. from shkiya." [<Aram. חלל (cavity)]

11

cha-lois (חלות) *n.* **1.** Instance of or concrete evidence in support of: INSTANTIATION. "Even if you're in the Beis Medrash, there's no C. of seder until 9:00 A.M." **2.** An instance representing the essence of an abstract principle: EXAMPLE. "This k'nas is a C. of Rebbe's new strict policy on attendance in shiur." [cf. chal]

chap (כאפען) *vt.* **1.** To grasp mentally: COMPREHEND. "Don't try to explain it to him; he never C. anyway." **2.** To grasp physically: GRAB. "He C. a second slice of pizza and ran before the cook could see him." **3.** To come upon suddenly, during some act: CATCH. "The manager C. the janitor going through the supply closet." **4.** To become occupied or involved with casually or unceremoniously: HAVE. "When I see the Menahel, I'll try to C. a shmooze with him about the leak in our dorm room." **5.** To obtain by chance or good fortune: GET A HOLD OF. "Baruch Hashem, just when I needed to go to New York, I managed to C. a ride." **6. chap ois, a.** To take before someone else has the opportunity to do so: GET. "I reached for the only copy of the sefer, but he C. it ois." **b.** To take in anticipation of someone else intending to do so: BEAT TO IT. "I reached for the sefer, but he C. me ois." *vt. & vi.* **7.** To pay attention to the existence of: NOTICE. "I had lost my wallet, but I didn't C. until I needed my phone card." *vi.* **8. chap arain,** To make use of or to utilize within limited parameters; to seize an opportu-

nity: TAKE ADVANTAGE, CARPE DIEM. "There's finally something decent for dinner. Make sure to C. arain." **9. chap it,** To be punished or reprimanded: GET IT. "He C. it from his parents when they saw his poor grades." **10. chap hispailus,** *Var. of* mispoyel. *n.* **11.** An instance of apprehending the true nature of something, particularly through intuitive understanding: INSIGHT. "His reputation as a good learner results from one or two good C. he had years ago." **12.** An ingenious expedient or technique: TRICK. "His C. first made him a lot of money and later landed him in jail." [<Yid. <Ukrainian хапати(grab)]

cha-shi-vus (חשיבות) *n.* **1.** An instance of noteworthiness: PRESTIGE. "It's a C. to sit by the mizrach-vant." **2.** Importance: SIGNIFICANCE. "We hope this work points out the C. of Yeshivish." [cf. machshiv]

cha-shuv(e) (חשוב) *adj.* **1.** Noteworthy and influential: EMINENT. "The Menahel has a C. position in the yeshiva." **2.** Dignified or elegant: DISTINGUISHED. "He looks really C. in his new Shabbos suit." **3.** Widely recognized for excellence: NOTED. "Willy Mays is a C. name in baseball." **4.** Having an excellent reputation: PRESTIGIOUS. "Central Park is a C. neighborhood." **5.** Superior and exclusive: CHOICE. "I've heard that caviar is eppis a C. food." **6.** Noteworthy or creating an impression: REMARKABLE. "It's C. to finish the whole seder Mo'ed in Elul zman." **7.** Brilliantly outstanding for actions, achievements, etc.: ILLUSTRIOUS. "Our most C. talmid knows Shulchan Aruch by heart." [cf. machshiv]

chav-ru-sa (חברותא) *n.* The person with whom one studies religious texts: FRIEND. "My C. and I finally finished the amud." [<Heb. חבר (join)]

chav-ru-sa-shaft (חברותאשאפט) *n.* A specific shared interest, or specifically that of chavrusas: ASSOCIATION. "My kid brother has been hanging around with that boy next door, and I don't approve of the C." [cf. chavrusa + cf. shaf]

cha-yav (חייב) *p.a.(t)* Modal auxiliary verb indicating necessity or compulsion: HAVE. "No matter what you think, you're C. to show some loyalty to your boss." [cf. choiv] **Var.** mechuyav.

cha-za-ka (חזקה) *n.* **1.** A pattern of past actions or events leading to the assumption of an extension of the same pattern in the future: HISTORY. "I'm not lending you another pen. You have a C. of not returning them." **2.** The belief, based on general experience, in the likelihood of something: PRESUMPTION. "There's a C. that everyone needs to feel safe and protected." [<Heb. חזק (strength)] —**N.B.** The form "chezkas" modifies a noun and creates the genitive case of "chazaka," i.e., "a chazaka of (being),"

i.e., "chezkas kashrus," "chezkas bari," and the like.

cha-zer (חאזר'ן) *vt.* To go over: REVIEW. "He C. his notes to get ready for the farher." [<Heb. חזר (return)]

cha-zir (חזיר) *n., pl.* **chazeirim** An uncouth, ill-mannered person: PIG. "That C. stayed by the kiddush until the last piece of herring." [<Heb. (swine)]

cha-zo-ra (חזרה) *n.* A second or repeated treatment or study: REVIEW. "The farher came after there was enough time for C." [cf. chazer]

chef-tza (חפצא) *n.* **1.** Reference to any concrete noun: THING. "Can I borrow your C. so I can hear this tape?" **2.** An object of some weight, gravity, or importance: SOMETHING! "This tape recorder has more switches than I can figure out how to use. It's a real C. (really something)." [<Heb. חפץ (want)]

che-lek (חלק) *n., pl.* **chalokim 1.** An essential or integral attribute or quality: COMPONENT. "A sense of humor is a C. of a healthy personality." **2.** An allotted portion: SHARE. "It's not that I like how it tastes so much. It's just that I have a C. in the company." *vi.* **3. have a chelek,** To partake or to have a share: PARTICIPATE. "If you had a C. in the mitzva, I'm sure you'll receive the s'char." [<Heb. חלק (part)]

chep-per (טשעפּרען) *vt.* **1.** To disturb in a persistent, irritating manner: PESTER. "The annoying new bochur relentlessly C. the older bochrim by hiding their seforim." *vi.* **2.** To manipulate or tinker with in order to operate or adjust: FIDDLE. "To get into the kitchen after curfew, the bochrim had to C. with the lock." **3.** To banter; to joke around: KID. "It looks like my roommate and I are fighting, but we just like to C." [<Yid. <Russian ущипнуть (pinch)]

chesh-bon (חשבון) *n., pl.* **cheshboinos 1.** Set of premises justifying a consequential action, statement, response, etc.: RATIONALE. "I can't see your C. for taking stamps from the yeshiva office without paying." **2.** Factors weighed and compared to reach a conclusion or decision: CONSIDERATION, DELIBERATION. "The Beis Medrash was not constructed arbitrarily; it was designed with a C." **3.** A predetermined course of action: PLAN. "I don't intend just to get in the car and go. I have a whole C." **4.** The cause of some undue loss: EXPENSE. "I don't care if my chavrusa is no longer interested in learning if he doesn't battel at my C." **cheshbon ois, 5.** To apportion nearly precisely: FIGURE OUT, WORK OUT. "The yeshiva is so cheap, they C. ois every piece of kugel at one per bochur." [<Heb. חשב (think)]
—**N.B.** For def. 2., note the elision of the indefinite article when translated into English.

chev-ra (חברא) *Var. of* chabura, def. 2.

chez-kas (חזקת) **Cf.** chazaka.

chi-dush (חידוש) *n., pl.* **chidushim 1.** That which exists, but has not been known previously: DISCOVERY. "His C. in the gemara answered all the questions we had had." **2.** An enlightening or astonishing disclosure: REVELATION. "It's a C. to me that my son hasn't been doing his homework." **3.** That which is new or different: INNOVATION. "It was the Menahel's C. to put springs on the doors to keep them from banging" **4.** That which is original, ingenious, and creative: NOVELTY. "It was a C. for the yeshiva to serve meat two nights in a row." **5.** A significant thing to be noted or understood: POINT. "Rebbe just spent a whole hour to speak out Rashi; I don't see his C." [<Heb. חדש (new)]

chi-luk (חילוק) *n., pl.* **chilukim** That which is dissimilar or which distinguishes: DIFFERENCE. "The twins look alike, but there is a major C. between their personalities." [cf. chelek]

chi-so-ren (חסרון) *n., pl.* **chisroinos 1.** A disadvantageous feature: DRAWBACK. "The biggest C. in this job is the lack of vacation time." **2.** That which mars perfection: FLAW. "The only C. with the idea of going in two cars is that we can only get one car." [<Heb. חסר (lack)]

chi-yuv (חיוב) *n., pl.* **chiyuvim 1.** That which one must do by law or by religious dictate: DUTY. "You have a C. not to take someone's things even if you think he won't mind." **2.** That for which one is accountable and is within one's control: RESPONSIBILITY. "My mother said I have a C. to call my grandparents once a week." **3.** The owing of something due to a feeling of indebtedness, recognition, or ethics: OBLIGATION. "I have a C. to return the sefer I borrowed." [cf. choiv]

chi-zuk (חיזוק) *n.* Spiritual or emotional support: ENCOURAGEMENT. "The Mashgiach gave him some C. when he felt he wasn't progressing in his learning." [<Heb. חזק (strong)]

choch-ma (חכמה) *n.* **1.** Wit or applied intelligence: CLEVERNESS. "It was a tough farher, but his quick answers revealed his true C." **2.** Clever or cunning act: TRICK. "It's a C. to get away every year without an audit." **3.** Field of knowledge: SUBJECT. "Science is a broad C." **4.** Craft or art: SKILL. "Plumbing can be a useful C." [cf. chacham]

choi-lek (חולק) *p.a.(i)* To disagree or find fault: TAKE ISSUE. "He was C. on one praht of my chabura, but he criticized the whole thing." [<Heb. חלק (part)]
—**N.B.** In English, the preposition "with" may be more natural than "on."

choi-shed (חושד) *p.a.(i)* **1.** To imagine to be true or likely: SUSPICIOUS.

"Despite his claim, I am still C. that he used my shaver." *p.a.(t)* **2.** To imagine to be guilty: SUSPECT. "I am C. him of telling the Mashgiach about the microwave I kept in the dorm." [<Heb. חשד (suspect)]

choi-shesh (חושש) *p.a.(t)* **1.** Concerned over a realization: AFRAID. "I'm C. that someone has gone through my drawers." *p.a.(i)* **2.** Conscientious to take note of and to provide for: ALERT. "I have an extra pair of tefillin to be C. for the Rabbeinu Tam." [cf. chshash]
—**N.B.** For def. 2., "to" may be more natural than "for" in English.

choiv (חוב) *n., pl.* **choivos** That which must be paid: DEBT. "He has a C. of a hundred dollars from making stupid sporting bets with the younger bochrim." [<Heb. חוב (obligation)]

chotsh (כאטש) *adv.* Despite the disputability of a wider statement: AT LEAST. "If you're going to buy expensive clothes, C. buy nice ones." [<Yid. <Russian хоть (although)]

chshash (חשש) *n., pl.* **chshushos 1.** A feeling of suspicion or apprehensive uneasiness: QUALM. "I have a C. that he used my tape recorder." **2.** A vague idea: INKLING. "From the smell, I have a C. that there are sardines for lunch." **3.** A cause for some attention, worry, or care: CONCERN. "If you call a cab to go to the airport, you should have the C. that it may come late." [<Heb. חשש (feeling)]

chum-ra (חומרא) *n.* An instance of strict adherence to the letter of the law: LEGALISM. "Not to take coffee into the Beis Medrash is a C." [<Aram. <Heb. חמר (substance)]

chutz-pa (חוצפא) *n.* **1.** Unmitigated impudence or gall: NERVE. "It was C. for him to make the whole bus wait while he packed at the last minute." **2.** An audacious, rude, or insulting act: AFFRONT. "It was a big C. for him to claim that the teacher had graded the tests according to personality." [<Aram. <Heb. חצף (effrontery)]

come on to *vt. (phrasal)* **1.** To employ when other options are unavailable: UTILIZE, RESORT TO. "If my parents say I can't go, I won't need to C. more complicated excuses for missing the concert." **2.** To bother as a last resort: IMPOSE UPON. "It's only that my taxi hasn't arrived that I've decided to C. you for a ride." [<Eng.]

come out *vi. (phrasal)* **1.** To culminate in a decision: CONCLUDE. "After a whole discussion, the hanhalla C. that the yeshiva should hold a second parlor meeting." **2.** To issue in a result: WORK OUT. "From what I see, it C. that this is essentially a machloikes rishoinim." [<Eng.]
—**N.B.** The phrase "kumt ois" is synonymous with the phrase "it comes out," def. 2.

come to *modal verb conjugated, followed by infinitive* To be in a situation wherein a consequential danger exists: HAPPEN, INADVERTENTLY. "Don't sit next to him on the bus, because you might C. speak lashon hara." [<Eng.]

Coun-try *n.* A resort area in a mountain range in Eastern New York State: CATSKILLS. "I think the C. is closer to here than the Adirondacks are." [<Eng.]

D

da-as (דעת) *n.* **1.** Normal, native intelligence: COMMON SENSE. "Running on the ice with Shabbos shoes shows a basic lack of D." **2.** Educated opinion: WISDOM. "I've seen the basic sugyos, but before I pasken, I wanted to see whether you have any D. on the subject." [<Heb. ידע (know)]

dacht zich (דאכטען זיך) *adv.* To the best of one's knowledge: (APPROPRIATE SUBJECT PRONOUN) THINK(S). "He said that, D. that company lost its hechsher, but he can't be sure." **Var.** duch zich.

da-her (דערהער) *n.* A unique or less than obvious rendering of a text: PARAPHRASE, TWIST. "His vort by Shalosh Seudos was a cute D. in the first posuk." [<Yid. <HG hören (hear)]

dahn (is) *p.a.(t.&i.)* To evaluate or pass judgment upon: ASSESS. "You shouldn't be D. other people unless you know their circumstances." [<cf. din]

da-kus-dik(e) (דקותדיק) *adj.* Requiring discernment; delicate in meaning: SUBTLE. "His D. terutz was insufficient for such a bomb kashe." [<Emulative of Yid. <Heb דוק (sharp)]

da-led a-mos (א' אמות) *n.* **1.** Limited ken: EXPERTISE. "The Mashgiach is smart, but he has his D. You need to ask a poisek." **2.** A field or sphere of action, thought, land, etc., over which one has domain: TERRITORY. "My roommate can make all the noise he wants as long as he stays out of my D." [<Heb. ד' (fourth letter) + אמה (forearm)]

dar-shen (דרשענען) *vi.* **1.** To talk incessantly and foolishly: PRATTLE. "At night, my roommate D. for hours about whatever comes to his mind." **2.** To deliver a discourse: LECTURE. "My boss D. about the need for saving money on phone calls." *vt.* **3.** To read into by overly careful analysis: SCRUTINIZE. "My chavrusa D. the posuk so intensely that he found chidushim that Moishe Rabbeinu

17

could never have intended." [<Yid. <Heb. דרש (interpret)]

dav-ka (דווקא) *adv.* **1.** Definitely or exactly stated: SPECIFICALLY. "He D. takes ketchup, not mustard, with his franks." **2.** *Var. of* bedavka. [<Heb. דק (sharp)]

de-hai-nu (דהיינו) *conj.* **1.** Introducing in the apposite: MEANING. "He said he'll think about it, D. I'd better forget it." **2.** Introducing as a list: BEING. "The yeshiva has only two kinds of food D. bad and worse." [<Aram. דא (which) + הוה (be)]

de-rech (דרך) *n., pl.* **drachim 1.** Method used in setting about a task, problem, etc.: APPROACH. "The teacher's D. is to allow questions only at the end of class." **2.** The manner of living according to the spirit of the Torah: MORES. "Some kiruv programs have been successful at bringing people back on the D." **3.** Established practice: CONVENTION. "The D. in our yeshiva is to go in the street with a jacket but no hat." **4.** A personal approach on a matter or issue: POSITION. "My D. is to wear a hat even in the street." [<Heb. דרך (tread)]
—**N.B.** For def. 2., note the Yeshivish use of the English definite article.

der-mohn (דערמאנען) *vt.* To reference briefly or incidentally: MENTION. "He D. the building fund although it had little to do with the main point of his speech." [<Yid. <HG mahnen (remind)]

dim-yoi-nos (דמיונות) *n.* False beliefs, usually based on unlikely wishes or expectations: DELUSIONS. "He has such D. of marrying the Rosh Yeshiva's daughter." [cf. dimyon]

dim-yon (דמיון) *n.* Resemblance, likeness, or similarity, particularly to a mark of distinction: COMPARISON. "There is no D. between his Lincoln and my Toyota." [<Heb. דמה (image)]

din (דין) *n., pl.* **dinim 1.** A rule governing action: REGULATION. "This D. includes even the worst-case scenario." **2.** Part of a composite: COMPONENT. "Ownership and control are two different D. in the right to property." [<Heb. דן (judge)]
—**N.B.** For def. 2., the English preposition "of" may replace "in" in translation.

di-vai-le (דערווײַלע) *adv.* In the interim: MEANWHILE. "You start the Tosfos, and D. I'll finish the Daf Yomi." [<Yid. <HG mittlerweile (meantime)]

di-yuk (דיוק) *n., pl.* **diyukim 1.** An interpretation based on wording and/or context: OBSERVATION. "His D. in the Maharal was the basis for his sefer on Machsheves Yisroel." **2.** A logical conclusion based on wording and/or context: INFERENCE. "His D. in the way the package was addressed made him uncertain whether it was for him." [<Heb. דק (sharp)]

doi-che (דויחה) *p.a.(t)* **1.** To set aside because of a minor problem: REJECT. "He was D. my p'shat without even listening." **2.** To have priority over: OVERRIDE. "A Tanna's statement is certainly D. a Rishon's." **3.** To push off to a later time: POSTPONE. "I was D. my appointment with the dentist until after seder." [<Heb. דחה (push)]

doi-chek(e) (דויחק) *adj.* Regarding a statement or response, forced or labored: FARFETCHED. "The bochur refused to accept such a D. p'shat. He pressed the Rosh Yeshiva for a real answer." [<Heb. דחק (press)] **Var.** (As a p.a. with singular subject) a doichek *or* doichek (with plural subject)

doi-me (דומה) *p.a.(i)* Alike or comparable: SIMILAR. "A Lincoln is only D. to a Cadillac in price." [<Heb. דמה (image)]
—**N.B.** eino doime implies the opposite: INCOMPARABLE.

drei (דרייען) *vi.* **1.** To loiter or idle without purpose: HANG. "If he didn't D. around so much, he might make some sales." *vt.* **2.** To interpret words to conform to a preconceived idea: MANIPULATE. "He D. the text so much that his p'shat was more like Purim Torah." *n.* A text so manipulated as to indicate an unlikely rendering: IRONY, SATIRE. "His p'shat in the posuk was such a D. as to be almost comical." [<Yid. <HG drehen (turn)]

duch zich *Var. of* dacht zich.

E

ee (אי) *prefix* Negates the quality of Yeshivish adjectives and adverbs: UN-, NON-. "It's very E.-geshmak to have teeth extracted." [Aram. אי (if)]

ef-sher (אפשר) Possibly: PERHAPS. "E. he'll be here by five o'clock, but don't count on it." [<Heb. פשר (mitigate)]

ei-del(e) (איידעל) *adj.* **1.** Possessing qualities of politeness and displaying respect for the feelings of others: COURTEOUS. "We need an E. guy to ask the boss for permission to leave earlier for winter Shabbosim." **2.** Soft-spoken and lacking excitement in demeanor: GENTLE. "We need an E. person to be our new dorm counselor." [<Yid. <HG edel (noble)]

ei-dus (עדות) *n.* **1.** Testimony of witness: VERSION. "He gave his E. to his parents to get his friend off the hook." **2.** The establishment of truth or fact: PROOF. "The puddle on the floor was E. that the plumbing in the dorm was defective." **3.** One who can attest to what has taken place: WITNESS. "Because of my injuries, I'm E. that you should wear safety belts." [<Heb. עד (present)]

ei-ge-ne (אייגען) *adj., p.a.* **eigens** Of or pertaining to one's own: PERSONAL. "I wasn't satisfied with Rebbe's p'shat, so I offered an E. terutz." [<Yid. <HG eigen (own)]

ein ha-chi na-mi (אין הכי נמי) *conj.* Accepted for the sake of argument: GRANTED. "E. anyone can make kiddush, but it's more bekavodik if the Rav is moitzi the oilam." [<Aram. אין (yes) + הכי (thus) + נמי (also)]

ei-no doi-me (אינו דומה) cf. doime.

ei-sek (עסק) *n.* **1.** Conducts or transactions relating to others: CONCERN. "Chutzpa like his should be the parents', not the yeshiva's, E." **2.** A tedious process: ORDEAL. "Arranging the rental of the bus for everyone to get to the convention became more of an E. than it was worth." [<Heb. עסק (involve)]

21

ei-tza (עצה) *n.* **1.** An idea or thought offered for the consideration of another: SUGGESTION. "I hated to drive with people who offer an E. every five minutes." **2.** Opinion based on superior, authoritative knowledge: TIP. "Let me give you an E. Don't ask the Menahel for favors until he's had his coffee." **3.** A choice, or the opportunity to choose among possibilities: ALTERNATIVE. "I haven't done my homework. I have no E. but to cut class." **4.** Opportunity for success; possibility: CHANCE. "The only E. for him is to switch yeshivas and hope they don't check his transcripts too carefully." [<Heb. יעץ (advise)]

e-la mai (אלא מאי) *conj.* Conjunction indicating that a clause is the result of the incorrectness of a previous clause: SO . . . "If your svara were right, pigs would be kosher; E. you're wrong." [<Aram. אלא (rather) + מאי (what)]

e-mes (אמת) *n.* **1.** That which is true: TRUTH. "The mother demanded that her child speak only the E." **2.** The external world as it exists independently of perception: REALITY, ESSENCE. "It is importance to know the E. of Hashgacha Pratis." [<Heb. (truth)] **Var. for def.** 1 emes la'amita (implies greater emphasis).
—**N.B.** Def. 1 may assume the English definite article.

e-mes(e) (אמת) *adj.* **1.** In accordance with the truth: TRUE. "The odd story turned out to be E." *(never p.a.)* **2.**

Genuine and actual; being really such: AUTHENTIC. "An E. talmid chacham usually has outstanding midos as well." [cf. emes] **Var.** emesdik(e).

e-mes-dik (אמתדיק) *adv.* As a matter of fact: GENUINELY. "E. we want you to eat by us. We've even brought you a chair already." [cf. emes]

e-mes-dik(e) *Var. of* emes(e).

Eng-lish *n.* The entire curriculum of non-religious courses taken at the elementary- or high-school levels: SCHOOL. "I had such a headache from shiur that I didn't go to E." [<Eng.]
—**N.B.** In Yeshivish writing, this word is rarely capitalized.

ep-pis (עפעס) *n.* **1.** Something of insignificant or little value: A TRIFLE. "I gave the meshulach E. just to get him off my back." *adv.* **2.** To a certain extent: SOMEWHAT. "I'm E. busy, but I can talk to you for a few minutes." **3.** For some strange reason: INEXPLICABLY, ODDLY. "He had just gotten up from a nap, but he still seemed E. tired." *art.* **4.** Used before or in place of the English indefinite article: AT LEAST, ANY KIND OF. "Do you have E. a pen, even a cheap one, as long as it writes?" *adj.* **5.** A relatively small number of: SOME. "I hear noises at night. I think there are E. mice in the dorm." [<Yid. <HG etwas (something)]

er-lich(e) (עהרליך) *adj.* **1.** Free from fraud or deception: HONEST. "The E. secretary was trusted to take everyone's money to the bank." **2.** Showing deep straightforwardness, neither feigned nor affected: SIN-CERE. "He's E. in his offer to learn with you before Shachris." [<Yid. <HG ehrlich (honest)]

er-lich-keit (עהרליכקייט) *n.* **1.** Freedom from fraud or deception: HON-ESTY. "To handle the government aid programs, the yeshiva would only take someone known for his E." **2.** Depth of straightforwardness, neither feigned nor affected: SINCERITY. "The bochrim felt comfortable talking to the Mashgiach because of his E." [cf. erlich(e)]

ersh-tins (ערשט) *adv.* In the first place: FIRST OF ALL. "E., I wasn't at the movies, and if I had been, it would be none of your business." [<Yid. <HG erstens (first)] **Var.** tzum ershtins.

e-tzem (עצם) *adj. (never p.a.)* **1.** Existing in reality or act: ACTUAL. "The E. physical fight was less violent than the verbal argument." **2.** Particular, mere, or utter: VERY. "The E. idea of vacation makes me daydream." *pron.* **3.** Having the essential nature of (used in the sense of the reflexive pronoun): ITSELF, THEMSELVES. "It's less the taste of the food here that bothers me than the E. quality." [<Heb. עצם (bone)]

—N.B. The English pronoun follows the noun.

F

fah-kert(e) (פערקעהרט) *adj.* On the contrary, being the opposite: BACK-WARD(S), OPPOSITE. "He was so stuck with a F. svara that he couldn't even listen to my taina." [<Yid. <HG umkehren (turn)]

fahr-tik(e) (פארטיג) *adj.* **1.** Finished or completed: DONE, READY. "As soon as the copies are F., I'll hand them out to all the offices." **2.** No longer available: GONE. "The pizza was F. before even half the bochrim had shown up." **3.** Being no longer relevant: BYGONE. "Don't bring up old arguments; it's a F. topic already." [<Yid. <HG fertig (ready)]

far-doost(e) *adj.* Lacking an element or characteristic: DEFECTIVE. "The lamp flickered because of the F., secondhand fixtures the yeshiva buys." [<Emulative of Yid. <HG das (that)]

far-her (פארהערן) *n.* **1.** Testing by constant, difficult questions: TRIAL, THIRD DEGREE. "When I walked in so late, the Mashgiach gave me a F. I'll never forget." *vt.* **2.** To test by careful, meticulous examination: INTERRO-GATE. "The cop F. me about the dent on my fender." [<Yid. <HG hören (hear)]

far-mah-tert (פערמאטערט) *(p.a. only)* Suffering from fatigue: EX-HAUSTED. "I can't drive back to yeshiva tonight; I'm F. from the chassuna." [<Yid. <HG müde (weary)]

far-nu-men (פערנומען) *adj. (p.a. only)* **1.** Active or involved: BUSY. "He was F. in the office all day and missed seder." **2.** In use: OCCUPIED. "All the showers were F., and I had to wait a long time." **3.** Absorbed in thought: PREOCCUPIED. "I was so F. before the final that I couldn't eat or sleep." **4.** Set aside or reserved for some purpose: TAKEN. "You can't use that shtender; it's F." [<Yid. <HG nehmen (take)]

far-shteit men (פערשטייט מען) *Var. of* farshteit zich.

25

far-shteit zich (פֿערשטײט זיך) *conj.*
Easy to see or understand; self-evi-
dent: OF COURSE, CERTAINLY.
"F. you should go to the chassuna
if you were invited." [<Yid.
<HG verstehen (understand) + sich (reflex-
ive pronoun)] **Var.** farshteit men.

far-shtunk-en(e) (פֿערשטונקען) *adj.*
Wretchedly bad: LOUSY. "I have an
old, F. car that rarely moves." [<Yid.
<HG stinken (stink)]

far-tracht (פֿערטראַכט) *adj. (p.a. only)*
1. Engaged in thought: PENSIVE.
"He is F. in that Tosfos and can't con-
centrate on anything else." **2.** Engrossed in contemplation about one's
own affairs: INTROSPECTIVE. "He
was F. before Rosh HaShana about the
past year." [cf. tracht ois]

fehlt (פֿעהלט) *adj.* Being deficient or
wanting in: LACKING. "The song is
nice, but F. harmony." [<Yid. <HG
fehlen (be missing)] **Var.** sfehlt, translated as: IT NEEDS.

ferd (פֿערד) *n.* Foolish or uncouth person: BOOR. "Don't pay attention to
his remarks; he just a big F." [<Yid.
<HG Pferd (horse)]

fer-en-fer (פֿערענטפֿערן) *vt.* **1.** To settle,
as in a problem: RESOLVE. "I am still
unable to F. all the stiros in my theory."
2. To declare free of blame: JUSTIFY.
"After he was thrown out of yeshiva,
he had to F. himself to his parents."
[<Yid. <HG antworten (answer)]

fer-gin (פֿערגינען) *vt.* Not to begrudge;
to be gracious about: GRANT. "I can
F. him his chavrusashaft with the
Kollel yungerman since I know his
parents pay for it." [<Yid. <HG
vergönnen (allow)]

fest(e) (פֿעסט) *adj.* Remarkably good:
EXCELLENT. "There was a F. lunch;
we tried to get doubles of everything."
[<Yid. <HG fest (firm)]

fier ois (פֿיהרן אויס) *vt. & vi.* To render
clear by further explanation through to
the end: ELUCIDATE. "It's not
enough to guess at an answer if you
can't F." [<Yid. <HG führen (lead) +
<Yid. אויס (out)]

fier zich (פֿיהרן זיך) *vt. reflexive* To behave according to one's personal demeanor or conduct: COMPORT ONE-
SELF. "He F. like an idiot when he got
drunk at the chassuna." [cf. fier ois +
<Yid. <HG sich (reflexive pronoun)]

fo-der (פֿאָדערן) *vt.* To cause or to involve necessarily as a consequence:
ENTAIL. "To get through the Daf
Yomi before Shachris F. a commitment." [<Yid. <HG erfordern (demand)]

fort (פֿאָרט) *adv.* Still, in spite of everything: NEVERTHELESS. "It may not
work, but I F. think we should try it."
[<Yid. <HG fort (still)]

frai(e) (פֿרײַ) *adj.* Not observant of
religious doctrine: IRRELIGIOUS.

"The F. guy came to shul on Shabbos, but he drove." [<Yid. <HG frei (free)]

freg (פרעגן) *vt.* To seek information: ASK. "He F. enough questions for all the teachers to be annoyed by him." [<Yid. <HG fragen (ask)]

fress (פרעסן) *vi.* To overindulge in eating: BINGE. "The musician F. at every chassuna he works at." [<Yid. <HG fressen (devour)]

frum(e) (פרומע) *adj.* Observant of the Torah's precepts: RELIGIOUS. "F. people should not even go in to such places." [<Yid. <HG fromm (pious)]

frum-kait (פרומקייט) *n., pl.* **frumkaiten** 1. Observance of the Torah's precepts: ORTHODOXY. "The Rabbonim have gathered to discuss the future of F. in America." 2. An observance considered stricter than normal: FANATICISM. "F. like his doesn't impress me; he only runs to learn when his parents have a job for him." [cf. frum(e)]

G

gad-lus (גדלות) *n.* **1.** A mark of superiority: DISTINCTION. "I bought the fanciest model, but I don't see its G." *adj. (p.a. only)* **2.** Remarkable for greatness: TREMENDOUS. "It's G. to finish Shas by the age of 20." [cf. gadol]

ga-dol (גדול) *n., pl.* **gedolim 1.** One who is notable to Jews for distinction of greatness: LUMINARY. "One must give kavod to every G." **2.** One who is exceptionally influential, talented, or successful at a given endeavor: WHIZ. "My brother is a G. at basketball." [<Heb. גדל (grow)]

gai-va (גאוה) *n.* Haughtiness or unseemly show of pride: ARROGANCE. "I wouldn't mind his success if he didn't have so much G." [<Heb. גאה (rise)]
—N.B. The term "ba'al gaiva" refers to one who displays qualities of gaiva: SHOW-OFF.

gantz (גאנץ) *adv.* **1.** To a sufficient degree: RELATIVELY, PRETTY. "It wasn't the fanciest chassuna, but the food was G. fine." **2.** To a great degree: EXCEEDINGLY, VERY. "That chassuna, with its nine-course meal, was G. expensive." [<Yid. <HG ganz (entire)]

gantz(e) (גאנץ) *adj.* Entire; complete: WHOLE. "He looks puny, but I once saw him down a G. pizza pie." [cf. gantz]

gash-mi-us (גשמיות) *n.* **1.** Indulgence in earthly pleasures: MATERIALISM. "It's real G. to eat steak every night." **2.** That which exemplifies materialistic values: CORPOREALITY. "The yevonim were shpitz G." **3.** That which contributes to bodily ease and pleasure: CREATURE COMFORTS. "The bochrim in that yeshiva must be pretty devoted to stay with such lousy G." [<Heb. גשם (rain)]

gash-mi-us-dik(e) (גשמיות-דיק) *adj.* Displaying or exemplifying concern for materialism: MATERIALISTIC. "Not every g'vir is G., but they are more likely." [cf. gashmius]

gav-ra (גברא) *n.* A person of worth and dignity: HEAVYWEIGHT. "Only a G. can walk into a new shul and take the amud." [<Aram. <Heb. גבר (strength)]

ge-der (גדר) *n., pl.* **gedarim 1.** Applicability of a definition to an act or circumstance: CLASSIFICATION, CATEGORY. "The Mashgiach decides what the G. of lateness to shiur is, not you." **2.** Qualification or restriction: LIMITATION. "If a bochur has no G., he is likely to be kicked out." [<Heb. גדר (fence)] **Var.** hagdara.

ge-feir-lich (געפעהרליך) *adv.* Unbelievably badly or intensely: HORRIBLY. "It was G. cold in the Beis Medrash. The bochrim went to learn in the dining room." [<Yid. <HG Furcht (fear)]

ge-feir-lich(e) (געפעהרליך) *adj.* Unbelievably bad or frightening: HORRIBLE. "I was late to the chassuna because of a G. traffic accident on the highway." [cf. gefeirlich]

geit-zich (גייטזיך) *vi. (imperative)* Leave me alone, and depart: GET LOST. "He cheppered me for an hour before I finally told him 'G.'" [<Emulative of Yid. <HG gehen (go)]

ge-kvetshed(e) (געקוועטשט) *adj.* Forcibly wrung or extracted: STRETCHED. "He wasn't ready for the Rosh Yeshiva's kashe, so he could only come back with a G. terutz." [<cf. kvetsh]

ge-noi (גענוי) *adv.* Exactly, just: PRECISELY. "I can't say G. what he did, but the Rosh Yeshiva sure was angry at him." [<Yid. <HG genau (exact)]

ge-shmak (געשמאק) *n.* **1.** Physical or intellectual joy or enjoyment: PLEASURE. "I get a lot of G. from listening to his drashos." *adv.* **2.** In a manner providing great satisfaction or pleasure: ENJOYABLE. "I don't know what he was talking about, but since he said it so G., I stayed to the end." [cf. shmek]

ge-shmak(e) (געשמאק) *adj.* Worthy of being relished: DELIGHTFUL. "His shiur was mamash G. He ferenfered every kashe beautifully." [cf. shmek]

ge-val-tik(e) (געוואלטיג) *adj.* Exceptional or remarkable: EXTRAORDINARY. "There was a G. response to the yeshiva's appeal for money." [<Yid. <HG gewalt (power)]

ge-zunt(e) (געזונט) *adj.* **1.** Having great force: POWERFUL. "The teacher gave him a G. slap for his chutzpa." **2.** Well and firmly constructed: STURDY. "The G. 1938 car hit the pole and wasn't even scratched." [<Yid. <HG gesund (health)]

ge-zunt-a-heit (געזונטהייט) *interj.* Response indicating that a matter is inoffensive: GO AHEAD, FREELY. "Smoke G., but open the window, please." [cf. gezunt(e)]

gir-sa (גירסא) *Var. of* nusach. [cf. goires]

give over *vt.* To tell; to present information for the purpose of giving an understanding: IMPART. "I'll try to G. the Mashgiach's shmooze without all the details." [<Eng.]

glatt(e) (גלאט) *adj.* Showing consistency of reason: SOUND. "His p'sak is based on a G. svara." [<Yid. <HG glatt (smooth)]

g-nai (גנאי) *n.* **1.** That which casts another in a bad light: DISPARAGEMENT. "Don't make excuses for me; I meant what I said as a G." **2.** That which one considers unsuitable for one's status, position, etc.: INDIGNITY. "It's a G. for the Rosh Yeshiva to wear such an old hat." [<Heb. גנה (disgrace)]

go bossur (go בתר) *vt.* To act, decide, or function in accordance with: FOLLOW. "If we can't agree, we'll just vote and G. the roiv." [<Eng. go + <Aram. בתר (after)]

goi-lem (גולם) *n.* A hopelessly foolish or ineffectual person: NUMSKULL. "That G. comes to Shachris every morning with his shirt on backwards." [<Heb. גלם (unformed matter)]

go-ing on *p.a.(t)* **1.** To refer to: MEAN. "When Rebbe said to go vaiter he was G. the Tosfos, not the Daf." **2.** To deal with or discuss: TREAT. "This Tosfos is G. the shveirkait in Rashi." **3.** To bear upon or concern: AFFECT. "When you say, 'Have a good day,' the adjective 'good' is G. the noun 'day.'" [<Eng.]
—N.B. Def. 2 may be more naturally translated as the preposition "about."

goi-rem (גורם) *p.a.(t)* **1.** To draw forth; evoke: ELICIT. "He was G. a lot of batulla with his constant jokes." *n.* **2.** That which serves to bring about an effect or result: CAUSE. "In the end the weather was the G. for canceling the trip." **3.** Cause, catalyst, driving force: IMPETUS. "He was the G. that the Mashgiach made the curfew earlier." [<Heb. גרם (cause)]
—N.B. Def. 3 is used as a predicate nominative and elides the English article.

goi-res (גורס) *p.a.(t)* **1.** To bring out the meaning of a text by imposing some variation in it: RENDER. "When I see a difficult Tosfos, I'm G. the words 'ask Rebbe' into the dibur hamaschil." **2.** To consider to be worthy of one's attention or care: REGARD, LISTEN TO. "I tried to ask the Rosh Yeshiva, but he wasn't G. me." [<Heb. גרס (text)]

gor (גאר) *adv.* **1.** To a noteworthy degree: VERY, QUITE. "Shiur was G. shveir; I barely chapped." *interj.* **2.** Expression of being impressed or amazed: OF ALL THINGS. "He didn't just rent any car. It's a Lincoln G." [<Yid. <HG gar (at all)]

gor·nisht (גארנישט) *n.* A shiftless, worthless person: GOOD FOR NOTHING. "He's a G.; I don't know why the yeshiva lets him stay." [<Yid. <HG gar nicht (not at all)]

grah·da (גראדע) *adv.* In reality; as a matter of fact: IT (SO) HAPPENS THAT. "G., the same guy who gives everyone musar is the one who took my pen and never returned it." [<Yid. <HG gerade (straight)]

greased out *Var. of* greasy.

greas·y *adj.* Fanatically, usually annoyingly, religious: EXTREME. "He's so G., he must have asked me fifty times whether he paid back the nickel he borrowed in 1973." [<Eng.] **Var.** greased out.

grois(e) (גרויס) *adj.* **1.** Complicated, intricate, hard to understand: COMPLEX. "He had a G. kashe on Rashi." **2.** Outstanding for size or for a specific quality: BIG. "He's a G. thief; count your money after he leaves your room." **3.** Of serious importance, influence, standing: EMINENT. "Everyone came to see the G. Rebbe." [<Yid. <HG gross (large)]

grubb(e) (גראב) *adj.* **1.** Fat or bulky: CORPULENT. "He's too G. to fit into his car." **2.** Coarse, inappropriate, and disgraceful: CRUDE. "He's too G. to make a good presentation in public." **3.** Having significant substance worthy of being savored: JUICY. "There's nothing like a G. steak." [<Yid. <HG grob (coarse)]

grubb·e (גראבע) *n.* A clumsy or unkempt person: SLOB. "I can't have such a G. for a roommate." [cf. grubb(e)]

gu·fa (גופא) *reflexive pronoun* **1.** Emphatic appositive for a noun: (APPROPRIATE REFLEXIVE PRONOUN). "I G. (myself) learned there, so I know all about that yeshiva." *adv.* **2.** Having a specific application: PARTICULARLY, EXACTLY, PER SE. "The notice was meant G. for the youngest bochrim." [<Aram. גופא (body, self)]

gut (גוט) *interj.* Generally favorable or commendable: OK, FINE. "G. you were unprepared for shiur; you can still make it up." [<Yid. <HG gut (good)]

gzei·ra (גזירה) *n.* An authoritative command either to perform or to refrain from performing a particular act; or an addition to a previously existing precept: INJUNCTION. "According to the G., you need to wait longer before you make havdala."

H

ha·a·ra (הערה) *n.* **1.** An instance of penetrating mental discernment: INSIGHT. "He usually paskens with a H. on the original sugya." **2.** A comment or observation: REMARK. "He's a big cynic and has a H. for everything." [<Heb. ער (awake)]

ha·cha·na (הכנה) *n.* A preparation or provision intended to facilitate an expected result: PRELUDE. "Going through all the psukim is just a H. to starting the sugya." [<Heb. כן (set, placed)]

ha·chun·nos (הכנות) *n.* **1.** Arrangements in advance: PLANS. "He was on the phone making H. for Bein HaZmanim." **2.** Measures taken to fulfill a condition: PROVISIONS. "He got a haircut to make H. for a shiduch." *vi.* **3. make hachunnos,** To prepare oneself: GET READY. "Stop making H. already, and get in the car." [cf. hachana]

haf·le·dik(e) (הפלא-דיק) *adj.* Very impressive, excellent: WONDER-FUL. "Shiur was H. I'm glad I taped it." [<Emulative of Yid. <Heb. פלא (wonder)]

ha·gam (הגם) *conj.* Disregarding the verity of: ALTHOUGH, IRRESPECTIVE OF THE FACT (THAT). "H. he lacked kavod, the Rosh Yeshiva liked him." [<Heb. גם (also)]

hag·da·ra *Var. of* geder.

ha gu·fa ra·ya *Var. of* haraya

hak·do·ma (הקדמה) *n.* That which precedes the main body: PREFACE. "Get to the point without the H., please." [<Heb. (first)]

hak·pa·da (הקפדה) *n.* **1.** Self-imposed stringency: INSISTENCE. "I have a H. to wear a gartel." **2.** Self-imposed ban or prohibition: RESTRICTION. "He has a H. on playing ball in Elul." [cf. makpid] *Var.* kepeida.

ha·le·vai (הלוואי) *conj.* Expressing a desire in the subjunctive mood: I WISH. "H. it snowed and I wouldn't

33

have to go to English today." [<Heb. לוה (accompany)]

ha-na-a (הנאה) *n.* **1.** Satisfaction from that which is to one's liking; enjoyment; delight: PLEASURE. "I get a lot of H. from my first cup of coffee." **2.** Helpful, valuable, or useful gain or profit: BENEFIT. "I lost my concession before I could get any H. from it." **3.** Practical employment or utility: USE. "If that's not your sefer, I don't think you should have any H. from it." [<Heb. נאה (pleasing)]

ha-na-cha (הנחה) *n.* Postulate, assumption, or proposition: PREMISE. "The whole H. that the yeshiva should provide the balebatim with chavrusas is wrong." [<Heb. נוח (rest)]

hand-l (האנדלען) *vi.* **1.** To argue persuasively for one's benefit: NEGOTIATE. "He always H. with his teachers for a few extra points." **2.** To deal competently with adversity: COPE. "He's finally learned how to H. with the headaches of dorm life." **3.** To negotiate and care for oneself dynamically: WHEEL AND DEAL. "This guy gets checks from three different Kollels and never shows up for seder. He really knows how to H." [<Yid. <HG Handel (trade, transaction)]

hand-ler (האנדלער) *n.* One who negotiates dynamically: WHEELER-DEALER. "He's such a good H., he sold five million American-made tacos to Mexico." [cf. handl]

ha-ra-ya (הראיה) *interj.* Response indicating that a statement has proven a previous proposal: THAT PROVES IT. "You can't be trusted with money. H. you've never paid me back the money you borrowed, and you're already asking for more." [cf. raya] **Cf.** veharaya.

har-tzig(e) (הערצליך) *adj.* Sincerely emotional and moving the heart: HEARTFELT. "He sang the nigun again and again because he found it so H." [<Yid. <HG herzig (hearty)]

ha-sa-ga (השגה) *n.* An impression or assumption: IDEA. "The new bochur had no H. just how strict the yeshiva is." [Heb. נסג (capture)]

ha-sa-gos (השגות) *n.* An ambition or desire to achieve, or the target of that desire: ASPIRATIONS. "The young Rebbe had H. of becoming a Rosh Yeshiva." [cf. hasaga]

has-cha-la (התחלה) *n.* A first attempt, move, etc.: START. "I didn't make it through the Daf, but at least I made a H." [<Heb. חלל (stir)]

hash-ka-fa (השקפה) *n., usually pl.* **hashkafos** System of guiding principles: PHILOSOPHY. "Before you leave yeshiva to go to work, be sure you have your H. clear in your mind." [<Heb. שקף (view)]

hash-pa-a (השפעה) *n.* **1.** Effect or consequence: INFLUENCE. "Just walking in the city can have a bad H. on you." **2.** The source for a change in one's actions: MOTIVATING FORCE. "My brother's encouragement was a real H. for me to learn more." [cf. mashpia]

has-ka-ma (הסכמה) *n.* **1.** Expression of consent or agreement: APPROVAL. "The Menahel had to give his H. before the bochrim could use the kitchen." **2.** A letter of approbation: COMMENDATION. "He persuaded the Rosh Yeshiva to write him a H. for his new sefer." [cf. maskim]

hatz-lo-cha (הצלחה) *n.* **1.** Attainment of a favorable end as a result of effort and talent: SUCCESS. "He had real H. in his learning and gained the respect of the other bochrim." **2.** Attainment of excellence, wealth, power, etc., as a result of good fortune: LUCK. "He has real H. in his new business and made millions in just months." [<Heb צלח (aim)]

ha-va-mi-na (הוה אמינא) *n.* **1.** That which is supposed with or without grounds: ASSUMPTION. "My H. was that I could get away with it without getting caught." **2.** A fleeting thought: DREAM. "I once had a H. to go around the world by boat and train." **3.** An explanation or reasoning behind a statement or action: RATIONALE. "What was your H. when you yelled at the Mashgiach?" **4.** Presumption or inkling: SUSPICION. "The check was a real surprise; I never had

a H. that anyone had collected money to help me out." [<Aram. הוה (be) + אמן (say)]

ha-yi-to-chen (היתכן) *conj.* Expresses wonder as to the probability of a given conception: COULD IT BE. "H. we're having shiur on Taanis Ester?" [<Heb. תכן (contain)]

hear *vt.* **1.** To comprehend fully: UNDERSTAND. "Trust me, I H. your taina; I just think you're wrong." **2.** To express understanding and assent: WOULD BUY THAT. "Rebbe's only response to my svara was 'I H.'" *vt.* **3.** To discern the makings or beginnings of: SENSE. "Although I haven't given the shaila much thought, I'm already starting to H. a possible terutz." [<Eng.]

hech-er(e) (העכער) *adj.* Mysterious, obscure, and esoteric due to an association with mystical or deeply spiritual matters: ARCANE. "He's so into H. things that he sometimes forgets to eat." [<Yid. <HG hoch (high)]

hech-rach (הכרח) *n.* Undeniable proof or need: IMPERATIVE, PROOF. "The New York plates are no H. that this bus is going to New York." [<Heb. כרח (force)]

hef-ker (הפקר) *adj.* **1.** Ownerless and free to take: UNENCUMBERED. "My old seforim are H., so take what you want." **2.** Utterly without order: CHAOTIC. "Once the bochrim showed up, the sheva brachos turned H." **3. make hefker** To renounce a claim upon: RELINQUISH. "If you've made your seforim H., put them here so others can take them." **4.** *Var. of* hefkerus. [<Heb. פקר (uproot)]

hef-ke-rus (הפקרות) *n.* A state of anarchy or chaos: DISORDER. "The lack of supervision caused the dorm to sink into H." [cf. hefker] **Var.** hefker, hefker velt.

hef-ker velt (הפקר וועלט) *Var. of* hefkerus.

hef-sed (הפסד) *n.* Detriment, disadvantage, or deprivation from failure to get, have, or keep: LOSS. "It was a big H. for me when my chavrusa left; I haven't found anyone else as good." [cf. mafsid]

hei-cha tim-tza (היכא תימצי) *n.* **1.** Method used to attain an end: MEANS. "I'd like to get to New York, but I have no H." **2.** Contrivance or device: EXPEDIENT. "I need some H. to listen to this new tape." **3.** Plausible case or sequence of events: SCENARIO. "I hear the svara behind the din, but I can't imagine any H. where it would apply." [Aram. היכא (where) + מצא (find)]

heim-ish(e) (היימיש) *adj.* **1.** Conveying an intense sensation of the warmth of Orthodox Judaism to one who recognizes it: WARM. "Just the smell of chulnt was enough to create a H. feel-ing." **2.** At ease; at home: COMFORTABLE. "The bochrim felt H. enough by the balebatim to help themselves to anything in the fridge." [<Yid. <HG heim (home)]

heis-dus (הייסט דאס) *interj.* Expressed otherwise: IN OTHER WORDS. "I'm tired and overworked. H., I need a vacation." [<Yid. <HG heissen (call) + das (that)]

hem-shech (המשך) *n.* **1.** The continuation or remaining part: REST. "The first chelek of the shiur was interesting enough to go back tomorrow for the H." **2.** The mutual relation of multiple components: CORRELATION. "I hear both parts of the taina, but I can't see the H. between them." [<Heb. משך (pull)]

he-ter (היתר) *n., pl.* **heterim 1.** Authoritative halachic capacity to permit: LICENSE. "If you want to take it easy, ask the Rabbi who gave me a H. when I asked." **2.** That which technically excuses a questionable act: JUSTIFICATION. "I think my dentist's appointment is a H. to leave seder a little early." **3.** Permission to perform a specifically predetermined act: DISPENSATION. "Because of his skin condition, he has a H. to shave during sefira." [cf. matir]

hez-ber (הסבר) *n.* That which clarifies or elucidates: EXPLANATION. "I once heard a H. of that sugya, but I don't think I could say it over." [cf. mazbir]

hish-tad-lus (השתדלות) *n.* Personal contribution, involvement, and efforts toward a goal: INITIATIVE, EFFORT. "He got a decent grade for his H., not for his research." [<Heb. שדל (effort)]

his-la-ha-vus (התלהבות) *n.* Zeal or fervor about a specific endeavor: ENTHUSIASM. "If you start the Daf with some H., you won't lose interest." [<Heb. להב (flame)]

his-pai-lus (התפעלות) *n.* **1.** Mild sense of being impressed: APPRECIATION. "I have a certain H. about how they can throw those bottles around without breaking any." **2.** Overwhelming feeling of reverence or of being impressed: AWE. "I had real H. watching them build the whole dorm in just a month." [cf. mispoyel]

hock (האקען) *vt.* **1.** To bother incessantly: ANNOY. "I H. the Mashgiach until he finally let me go home for Shabbos." **2.** To pose constant questions: ASK. "He's not shy; he'll H. Rebbe until he's satisfied with the answer." *vi.* **3.** To speak or say quickly, incoherently, and incessantly: JABBER. "He H. about the politics all day, but never even reads the paper." *vt.* **hock up 4.** To prove wrong with a long, quickly paced argument: REFUTE. "The yungerman H. the shiur with some sharfe kashes." [<Yid. <HG hacken (chop)]

hold *vt.* **1.** To assert in the face of evidence or argument to the contrary: MAINTAIN. "I hold we should stay and learn even if it gets late." *adj. (conjugated as a verb in progressive tenses)* **hold by 2. a.** On the verge of: CLOSE TO. "With all that handshaking, I guess they're H. an agreement." *prep. (conjugated as a verb in progressive tenses)* **b.** Prepared or ready for, as in some innovation: UP TO. "The yeshiva office is just getting used to the copiers; they're not H. computers, yet." *vt.* **hold of 3. a.** To have congruence of opinion with: AGREE WITH. "I H. his p'sak, but his lomdus is shvach." **b.** To enjoy or find agreeable: LIKE. "I H. his smooth way of dealing with people." [<Eng.]

ho-ri-va (o-ver) (האריעווען) *vt.* **1.** To clarify through research: ANALYZE. "He sat down and H. the same Tosfos for hours." **2.** To dispute with others about an issue or quandary: DISCUSS. "They continued to H. shiur through lunch." **3.** To consider or think intently about: CONTEMPLATE. "It was only after he'd H. the shaila for hours that he found a terutz." [<Yid. <Slav. (work hard)]

ho-sa-fa (הוספה) *n.* **1.** That which adds to size: EXTENSION. "This was not lichatchila part of the Beis Medrash; it's a H." **2.** An enhancement or betterment: IMPROVEMENT. "The harmony was my H. to the nigun." *usually pl.* **hosafos 3.** Written or expressed remarks about something previously presented: COMMENTS, GLOSSES. "My paper came back with so many H., I'm surprised I got a grade for it." [cf. moisif]

I

i-kar (עיקר) *n., pl.* **ikarim 1.** The essential or principal part: CORE. "The I. of winning at baseball is probably the batting, not the pitching." *adj., usually* the ikar **2.** The most urgent or pressing: PRIMARY. "Do this Tosfos first since it's the I." **3.** Of the utmost importance: ESSENTIAL. "The I. point in that Tosfos is right in the middle." [<Heb. עקר (uproot)]

i-kuv (עיכוב) *Var. of* meakev, defs. 3 and 4.

i-lu-i (עילוי) *n. pl.* **iluyim** A person of high intelligence or ability: GENIUS. "From just one shiur, I'm zicher he's an I." [<Heb. עלה (rise)]

i-lu-yish(e) (עילויש) *adj.* Displaying characteristics of genius: BRILLIANT. "The pshat doesn't shtim with the girsa, but the svara is I." [cf. ilui]

in gantz-en (אין גאנצ׳ן) *adv.* To a total degree: ENTIRELY. "Now that the yeshiva doesn't even have good food,

it's I. worthless." [<Yid. <HG ganz (whole)]

in-tre-sant(e) (אינטערעסאנט) *adj.* Engaging or fascinating: INTERESTING. "It's I. that the yeshiva has an earlier curfew for the older bochrim than for the younger ones." [<Yid. <Fr. (interesting)]

in-yan (עניין) *n., pl.* **inyanim 1.** A subject of conversation: TOPIC. "If you're making a chabura, I can show you some gemaros on the same I." **2.** That which one's efforts are intended to attain or secure (generally of a religious nature): OBJECTIVE. "There's an I. to wear a hat when you daven. It's not just a style." [<Heb. ענה (answer)]

is-ser (איסור) *n., pl.* **issurim 1.** That which Jewish law prohibits: PROSCRIPTION. "There's an I. against eating meat with fish." **2.** A breach of Jewish law: OFFENSE. "It's an I. to talk lashon hara." [cf. asur]

39

i-yun (עיון) *n.* **1.** Examination of sources to develop a coherent, educated opinion: RESEARCH. "If you plan to say that chabura, you'd better hope no one did any I." **2.** Deep consideration or concentration: MEDITATION. "I can't give you an eitza without some I. first." [<Heb. עין (eye)]

K

kal va-cho-mer (קל וחומר) *adv.* **1.** With assuredness of mind or action based on an earlier, more restrictive, premise; assuredly; certainly: INDUBITABLY. "I can zicher finish the mesechta by Thursday and K. by Shabbos." *n.* **2.** Assumption on the basis of a previous, more severe instance: EXPERIENCE. "I stay away from their fleishige stuff because of a K. from our shailos on their parve stuff." [<Heb. קל (light) + חמר (substance)]

ka-ma (כמה) *adj.* Several; quite a number of: NUMEROUS. "He's been through hilchos Shabbos K. times and occasionally paskens shailos." [<Heb. כמה (how many)] **Var. with additional emphasis** "kama vekama."

ka-no-i (קנאי) *n.* One who thinks or behaves zealously: FANATIC. "He's such a K. for his Rosh Yeshiva that it doesn't even pay to mention what other gedolim have to say about it." [cf. mekanne]

ka-no-us (קנאות) *n.* A fervent feeling or act of zealousness: PARTISANSHIP. "His K. wouldn't let him sit still while people made fun of his Rebbe." [cf. mekanne]

ka-no-us-dik(e) (קנאות-דיק) *adj.* Unswervingly zealous: FERVENT. "His K. musar gives some real chizuk, but its goals are a little unrealistic." [cf. mekanne]

kan-sen (קנס׳נען) *vt.* To impose a penalty or fine upon: PENALIZE. "Rebbe K. me ten Mishnayos B'al Peh for eating during shiur." [<Yid. cf. knas]

kash-e (קשיא) *n.* A question posing some difficulty because of apparent inconsistencies with accepted premises: PROBLEM. "It's no K. how the Rosh Yeshiva's nephew got accepted to the yeshiva despite his shvache learning." [<Aram. קשי (hard)]

ka-va-na (כוונה) *n.* **1.** Attention to the meaning, spirit, and purpose of words: INTENTION, PURPOSE. "If you just

41

spoke your mind, I wouldn't have to guess at your K." **2.** Intensity and sincerity of emotion: PASSION, FEELING. "He made his appeal with such K. that I doubled my gift to the yeshiva." [<Heb. כן (set)]
—**N.B.** In reference to davening, "kavana" connotes both meanings simultaneously.

ka-va-ya-chol (כביכול) *adv.* In recognition of the figurative or anthropomorphic nature of a description: METAPHORICALLY. "K., Hashem feels the pain of every Jew who suffers." [<Heb. יכל (able)]

ka-vod (כבוד) *n.* **1.** Honor or show of respect: DEFERENCE. "The Mashgiach was concerned that the younger bochrim gave so much K. to the older boys who wore expensive clothes and rented luxury cars." **2.** A special right granted as an honor: PRIVILEGE. "The older boys convinced the younger bochrim that it's a K. to put away all the seforim after seder." [cf. mechabed]

ke-dai (כדאי) *adj.* *(p.a. only)* **1.** Lucrative; bringing about remunerative gain: PROFITABLE. "In the end, it turned out to be K. to run the candy machines in the dorm." **2.** Effecting some personal benefit: ADVANTAGEOUS. "If you want good chavrusas, it's K. to sit near the Mashgiach." **3.** Valuable in any way: WORTH IT. "When you go to Toronto for the chassuna, it's K. to stop and see Niagara Falls." [<Aram. די (enough)]

ke-di-mus (קדימות) *n.* The right to prior attention due to rank or superiority: PRIORITY. "Rebbe was last to arrive, but went first because he had K." [<Emulative of Heb. קדם (first)]

kei-lim (כלים) *n.* The ability to perform well with one's given powers or potentials: FACULTIES. "When I see my roommate change his mood so unexpectedly, I thinks he's lost his K." [<Heb. כלי (vessel)]

ke-i-lu (כאלו) *conj.* As if it were that: AS THOUGH. "My chavrusa attacked my svara K. I was the biggest idiot in the world." [<Heb. -כ (like) + אלו (if)]

ke-ne-ged (כנגד) *prep.* **1.** In opposition to: AGAINST. "He spoke out K. the new, transparent mechitza in the local shul." **2.** Representative or symbolic of: FOR, ABOUT. "Rebbe had thirty questions on the test, one K. each Tosfos the shiur had learned." [<Heb. נגד (facing)]

ken zain (קען זיין) *adv.* Being within the limits of ability, capacity, or realization: POSSIBLY. "Although I have to go out of town, K. I'll be back in time for shiur." [<Yid. <HG können (able) + sein (be)]

ke-pei-da (קפידא) *Var. of* hakpada.

ke-se-der (כסדר) *adv.* **1.** Steadfastly adherent to the same principles, courses, behaviors, etc.: CONSTANTLY. "My roommate bothers

me K., and I can't get enough sleep."
2. Continuously and interminably in the same course of action: PERSISTENTLY. "He K. asks dumb questions just to annoy the teacher." **3.** By the usual way of acting in given circumstances: CUSTOMARILY. "He goes to the country K. as long there's Bein HaZmanim." [cf. seder]

ke-se-der-dik(e) (כסדרדיק) *adj.* Recurrent or constant: PERENNIAL. "The banging pipes in the dorm are a K. shter to my sleep." [cf. seder]

ke-sher (קשר) *Var. of* shaichus, defs. 1, 3, 4, and 6. [<Heb. קשר (knot)]

ki-di-bu-i (כדבעי) *adv.* **1.** In a careful or thorough manner: PROPERLY. "The appeal letter was written K., and the yeshiva received a lot of donations in response." **2.** Having all the characteristics: BY DEFINITION, DEFINITIVELY. "That poor bochur was meshuga K. and wound up in an institution." *adj.* **3.** In order: PROPER. "If his notes were K., he would have done better on his farher." [<Aram. בעי (desire)]

ki hu zeh (כי הוא זה) *n.* **1.** A small amount (as in "at all"): IOTA. "I don't have a K. of kavod for someone who learns all day and speaks lashon hara all night." **2.** Even a small amount: THING. "I wouldn't give him a K. for his beat-up, old car." [<Heb. כי (rather) + הוא (this) + זה (it)]

kim-at (כמעט) *adv.* Almost or nearly: PRACTICALLY. "I'm still hungry, because there was K. nothing to eat for lunch." [Heb. מעט (little, few)]

ki-ruv (קירוב) *Nominative form of* mekarev.

kish-roi-nos (כשרונות) *n.* Marked potential and capability: TALENT. "The tall first bochur discovered his basketball K. in summer camp." [<Heb. כשר (proper)]

ki-tzur (קיצור) *n.* Summary or précis: DIGEST. "That tshuva is only a K. of the whole shiur that appears in the chidushim." [cf. mekatzer]

klal (כלל) *n., pl.* **klullim 1.** A fixed rule: PRINCIPLE. "There is a K. behind all the yeshiva's policies." **2.** A generally accepted rule: GUIDELINE. "As a K., you should go and get all the seforim you'll need before you sit down for seder." [<Heb. כלל (include)]

kla-pei (כלפי) *prep.* As regards; as related to: CONCERNING. "He only feels chashuv K. the younger bochrim." [<Aram. כלפי (facing)]

kleir (קלערען) *vi.* **1.** To accept for the moment: POSIT, THINK. "Right now, I'm K. that he should take the car since it looks pretty clean." **2.** To think carefully about in order to reach a decision: CONSIDER. "I'm K. to buy my own Ritva, since Rebbe speaks it out so often." **3.** To contemplate, deliberate, or reflect upon in order to select among options: DEBATE. "I'm K. whether to buy a car or to get by with the buses." *n.* **4.** A first thought: CONSIDERATION. "I had a K. to go to the chassuna, but I didn't want to cram into the back seat." [<Yid. <HG klären (clarify)]

klop (קלאפען) *vi.* **1.** To strike and produce a noise in order to call attention: KNOCK. "The bochur K. on the table so the Rosh Yeshiva could speak." **2.** To work out well or to portend to do so: GO. "Sometimes a chavrusashaft makes good sense, but it just doesn't K." *n.* **3.** A knock as a call to attention: BANG. "We argued until we heard the K. for mincha." **4.** A hit or rap: BLOW. "He walked right into the door and got a painful K." [<Yid. <HG klappen (hit)]

kluhr (קלאר) *adv.* **1.** Explicitly; without a doubt: UNEQUIVOCALLY. "He told me K. that he wants to come along if there's room." **2.** With clarity and understanding: PERFECTLY, COLD. "He knows hilchos tfillin K; you can ask him your shaila." [cf. kleir] **Var. for def. 1** kluhr ois.

kluhr(e) (קלאר) *adj.* **1.** Unsullied; pure; clear: PRISTINE. "He walks miles every Erev Shabbos just to find a K. mikveh." **2.** Clearly expressed and easily understood: LUCID. "Rebbe's explanation was so K. that no one asked any questions." **3.** Explicit; openly stated: EXPRESS. "The Mashgiach

gave him a K. order to be back before noon." **4.** Manifest; evident; indubitable: OBVIOUS. "It's K. that he doesn't really want to learn with you. He just doesn't know how to tell you." **5.** Neither contestable nor questionable: INDISPUTABLE. "My raya was K., and my chavrusa didn't bother arguing his point." [cf. kleir]

kluhr ois (קלאר אויס) *Var. of* kluhr, def. 1.

knas (קנס) *n.* That which is imposed as a punishment for an offense: PENALTY. "The Mashgiach made his curfew earlier as a K. for disappearing during seder." [<Aram. קנס (fine)]

kneitsh (קנייטשען) *vt.* **1.** To make creases or folds in: CRUMPLE. "If you K. that bill, the machine won't take it." *vt. & vi.* **2.** To strain unnaturally; to force in an affected manner: WRENCH. "I K. a smile even though the Rosh Yeshiva shlugged up my pshat in front of everyone." *n.* **3.** A slight but clever variation: NUANCE. "If you listen carefully, you'll hear a lot of subtle K. in this tape." **4.** A sudden, unexpected change of course; or a novel treatment: TWIST. "To find a heter like you want takes a real K. in Hilchos Shabbos." [<Yid. <HG kneten (knead)]

ko-fu-i toi-va (כפוי טובה) *n.* One who displays a lack of thankfulness: INGRATE. "If you can talk to me like that after all I've done for you, you're a big K." [<Heb. כוף (bend) + cf. toiva]

koi-chos (כחות) *Var. of* koyach.

koi-dem kol (קודם כל) *adv.* In the first place: FIRST. "K. we'll finish the Daf Yomi. Then we talk about other plans for the day." [<Heb. קדם (before) + כל (all)]

koi-ne (קונה) *p.a.(t)* **1.** To assume controlling ownership or possession of: ACQUIRE. "To learn a Daf once isn't enough to be K. it unless you chazer it properly." **2.** To reach or fulfill the requirements of: ATTAIN. "He learned there long enough to be K. the title of 'eltere bochur.'" **3.** To gain a thorough knowledge or understanding of: APPREHEND. "I've been K. enough of the material to pass the Regents." [<Heb. קנה (buy)]

koi-vei-a (קובע) *p.a.(t)* **1.** To be persistent at: MAINTAIN. "He is K. his Daf Yomi so he wouldn't fall behind." **2.** To do with commitment and responsibility: UNDERTAKE. "He was K. his learning and had real hatzlocha." **3.** To set aside: RESERVE. "To do well in school, you have to K. time for homework." **4.** To establish or decide the specifications of: DETERMINE. "The Rosh Yeshiva was K. new times for seder during Summer Zman." **5.** To center or use as a focus: BASE. "If you are K. your lunch on pizza, you should wash for it." [<Heb. קבע (affix)]

ko-vu-a (קבוע) *adj. (p.a. only)* **1.** Firmly placed: FIXED. "That beam is

K. in the wall; you couldn't move it without tearing down the building." **2.** Established firmly: SET. "The yeshiva's rules about college were K., and there was no point arguing." [cf. koiveia]

koy-ach (כח) *n.* **1.** Physical power: MIGHT. "I don't think that skinny bochur has the K. to carry his own seforim." **2.** Power to judge, act, or command: AUTHORITY. "Only the Mashgiach has the K. to change the curfew for the dorm." **3.** Innate ability: FACULTY. "As long as he has the K. to communicate, I wouldn't assume him to be stupid." **4.** The resources for action: ENERGY. "I'm so tired that I don't even have the K. to brush my teeth and put on my pajamas." **5.** Ability for satisfactory performance: CAPACITY. "A fund-raiser needs to have the K. to speak publicly." [<Heb. כח (strength)] *Var. for defs.* **1, 4, and 5** koichos.

kratz (קראצען) *vi. also,* **kratz around 1.** To idle or waste time: TARRY, LINGER, HANG AROUND. "He K. so much getting ready to learn that seder is usually over before he sits down." *n.* **2.** A sharp desire or craving: YEN. "Yeshiva dinners give me a K. for home cooking." **3.** A sudden inclination: URGE. "The Menahel got a K. to kansen bochrim for leaving the lights on in the dorm rooms." [<Yid. <HG kratzen (scratch)]

krum(e) (קרום) *adj.* **1.** Irreverent or aberrant: DEVIANT. "His articles are so K. that the kehilla was afraid to take him as a Rav." **2.** Dishonest and lacking in integrity and uprightness: CROOKED. "Sometimes the yeshiva gets in trouble when it accepts donations from people who have K. businesses." **3.** Specious, spurious, illogical: WARPED. "The way he learned the sugya was so K. that it could have come from a priest." [<Yid. <HG krumm (bent)]

ku-la (קולא) *n.* A leniency based on subtle legality: LOOPHOLE. "He lived his life by so many K. that most people didn't even know that he was frum." [cf. meikl]

kumt ois (קומט אויס) *Var. of* come out, def. 2.

kuntz (קונץ) *n.* **1.** Originality or cleverness: INGENUITY. "There is no K. in buying the first item you see." **2.** A feat displaying ability or talent: SKILL. "It's a K. to balance a job, a family, and a few hours a day of learning." **3.** Planned, organized method for attaining a specific goal: STRATEGY. "The K. to winning this game is to protect pieces before going on the offensive." [<Yid. <HG Kunst (skill)]

kvetsh (קוועטשען) *vi.* **1.** To complain in a feeble, peevish way: WHINE. "The baby K. for milk all night." *vt.* **2.** To fill beyond a comfortable capacity: CRAM. "They all K. themselves into the compact car so they wouldn't have to pay to rent a bigger one." **3.**

To act upon with steadily applied weight or force: SQUEEZE. "The yeshiva is so stingy with milk that the bochrim K. the cartons to get every drop." **4.** To linger; to progress slowly or laboriously: DRAG. "I would enjoy the shiur more if Rebbe didn't K. for so long." **5. kvetsh out a.** To prolong; to lengthen in time: STRETCH. "He K. his speech to fill the forty-five-minute time allotment." **b.** To wring out an unlikely interpretation forcibly: EXTRACT. "He K. a pshat on a gemara from a Medrash." *n.* **6.** One who consistently expresses discontent: COMPLAINER. "The bochur is such a persistent K. that people usually give him what he wants just to shut him up." [<Yid. <HG <MFr esquasher (squash)] **Var. for def. 6** kvetsher.

kvetsh-er (קוועטשער) *Var. of* kvetsh, def. 6.

kvetsh-y (קוועטשענדיק) *adj.* Marked by the tendency to complain peevishly and feebly: CRANKY. "Don't ask the Mashgiach for reshus to go home until he's had his coffee and is less K." [cf. kvetsh]

kvi-us (קביעות) *n.* **1.** A serious undertaking: COMMITMENT. "He has a K. to learn two Mishnayos before shachris." **2.** Sense of stability: BASE. "The young bochur needed a K. and couldn't learn out of town." **3.** A regular manner: REGIMEN. "He has a K. that begins with waking up at 6:00 A.M. exactly." [cf. koiveia]

kvi-us-dik(e) (קביעותדיק) *adj.* **1.** Done with commitment: REGULAR. "He learns alone after the yeshiva's K. seder." **2.** Predetermined or established, as in time: SET. "He leaves for work at a K. time based on the bus schedule." **3.** Recurring regularly: CONSTANT. "His K. jokes caused the teacher finally to blow up at him." [cf. koiveia]

L

lam-dan (למדן) *n., pl.* **lamdunnim**
One who has both a broad ken and a
deep understanding of the Torah:
PRODIGY. "Reb Chaim in his sefer
showed what a real L. can accomplish." [cf. lomdus]

lav dav-ka (לאו דווקא) *adv.* **1.** Not
absolutely or exactly: NOT NECES-
SARILY. "I'm L. going with you. I
may just rent a car for myself." *adj.*
(p.a. only) **2.** Not of or by necessity;
not absolute or definite: QUESTION-
ABLE, UNCERTAIN. "It's L. that I'll
need to go to the store if I can scrape
together enough to eat here." **3.** Being
only nearly as specified: INEXACT,
APPROXIMATE. "The amounts on
this recipe are L." [<Aram. לאו (not)
+ cf. davka]

learn *vi.* **1.** To be involved in the acquisition of Torah knowledge through
reading and reflection, or to do so as
an occupation: STUDY. "I try to L.
whenever I have a chance." *vt.* **learn
out 2.** To conclude or derive on
sources: DEDUCE. "My Rebbe can L.

out chidushei Torah from observations
of nature." **learn up 3.** To acquire a
basic and general overview of a specific area of a Torah subject: PERUSE.
"I was late to seder, so I just L. up the
amud and ran to shiur." [<Eng. (emulative of Yiddish)]

learn-ing *n.* Comprehensive academic involvement in Torah study,
including as an occupation: SCHO-
LASTICS. "He hopes to stay in L. as
long as he can afford to." [<Eng.
(emulative of Yiddish)]

le-be-dik(e) (לעבעדיק) *adj.* Marked
either by life, vigor, and energy or
by activity, spirit, and excitement:
LIVELY. "You couldn't tell what a L.
guy he was until you saw him at camp
during Bein HaZmanim." [<Yid. <HG
lebendig (alive)]

le-be-di-kait (לעבעדיקייט) *n.* Vigor,
energy, etc.: LIVELINESS. "You
could see his L. on his face and in his
attitude." [cf. lebedik(e)]

49

le-ga-bei (לגבי) *prep.* In reference to; with respect to: REGARDING, CONCERNING. "L. whom will you feel embarrassed in that suit? No one will even notice." [<Aram. גב (beside)]

le-hach-is (להכעיס) *adv.* Filled with, prompted by, or showing malicious ill will to hurt or humiliate: SPITEFULLY, INTENTIONALLY. "I know that he broke the window L." [<Heb. כעס (anger)]

le-hach-is-dik(e) (להכעיסדיק) *adj. form of* lehachis: SPITEFUL. "Breaking the window was a L. attempt to cost me money." [cf. lehachis]

lein-ing (לייענען) *n.*, in the phrase **make a leining** A preliminary study of a sugya involving only a cursory understanding of it: OVERVIEW. "I didn't know what shiur would be about, so I just made a L. on the amud." [<Yid. <HG lesen (read)] **Var.** leinus.

lei-nus *Var. of* leining.

lei-tzo-nus (ליצנות) *n.* Scornful contempt, ridicule, derision: MOCKERY, FUN. "Once the boy discovered that everyone was making L. of him for paying so much attention to his homework, he felt he couldn't trust anyone." [<cf. letz]

le-maf-rei-a (למפרע) *adv.* **1.** Taking effect, as of a past occurrence: RETROACTIVELY. "The new tuition costs worked L., so my father had less money in the summer than he thought he would." **2.** With the recognition afforded by hindsight: RETROSPECTIVELY. "L., I realize that my son would have learned better out of town." [<Aram. Heb. פרע (uncover)]

le-mai-se (למעשה) *conj.* **1.** Clausal introduction implying insight or knowledge: THE FACT IS THAT. "L., you're wrong. You can talk till you're blue in the face, but, L., you're wrong." *adv.* **2.** In reality: PRACTICALLY SPEAKING. "I don't need to hear your whole cheshbon. L., are you coming with us or not?" **3.** Actually: COME TO THINK OF IT. "L., now that I hear your cheshbon, I think you're right." *adj.* **4.** Suitable for actual use: PRACTICAL. "A wild tie like that just isn't L. for yeshiva." *vi.* **come lemaise 5.** To become actual fact: MATERIALIZE. "The shiduch was a good idea, but it just never came L." [<Heb. עשה (do)]

le-mas-ka-na (למסקנה) *adv.* **1.** At last: FINALLY. "We had a flat on the way to the chassuna, but L. we arrived." **2.** All said and done: ULTIMATELY. "Don't give me all the details; L., did you shaf a car or not?" [cf. maskana]

le-shoi-nos (לשונות) *n.* An interjectory word or expression, deemed profane or inappropriate: EXPLETIVE(S). "In our yeshiva, even the secular teachers won't allow any L. in the classroom." [cf. loshon]

letz (לץ) *n., pl.* **letzim 1.** A person with (generally inappropriate) characteristics of high spirits, gaiety, and humor in action or speech: JOKER. "The bochur was smart but a big L. He never took anything seriously enough to be matzliach." **2.** One who makes flippant, commonly sardonic remarks or retorts, due mostly to a lack of maturity: WISEACRE. "For his own good, I wouldn't let that L. meet the Rosh Yeshiva." [<Heb. לצץ (scoff)]

li-chat-chi-la (לכתחילה) *adv.* **1.** Occurring at the beginning; at first: INITIALLY. "L. we were going to learn Bava Kama, but we decided to learn Bava Basra with everyone else." **2.** Done in the best possible way: OPTIMALLY. "L., you should try to learn far from the door, so you don't get distracted by people coming in and out." **3.** To begin with: ALTOGETHER. "If I'd known there would be so much fighting, I wouldn't have mentioned it L." [<Aram. <Heb. התחילה (begin)]

li-chat-chi-la-dik(e) (לכתחילה-דיק) *adj.* Most favorable or advantageous: OPTIMAL. "The L. way to get good grades is to study hard." [cf. lichatchila]

lich-o-ra (לכאורה) *adv.* **1.** Seemingly as such while allowing for the possibility of the opposite: APPARENTLY, OSTENSIBLY. "L. I should take the day to do my laundry. I can't stand all these socks lying around my room." **2.** Able to be taken for granted; assumed true in the absence of proof

to the contrary: PRESUMABLY. "It's already ten o'clock. L. he should be in Lakewood by now." [<Aram. <Heb. אור (light)]

lo yitz-lach (לא יצלח) *Var. of* nebbach. [cf. hatzlocha]

loit (לויט) *prep.* In accord with the methodology of; as stated by: ACCORDING TO. "L. the Pnei Yehoshua, the Maharsha's kashe doesn't begin." [<Yid. <HG laut (according to)]

lom-dish (למדיש) *adv.* With logic; according to reason or sound judgment while following a complicated train of thought: LOGICALLY. "He learned up the sugya so L. that only the best bochrim could follow." [cf. lomdish(e)]

lom-dish(e) (למדיש) *adj.* **1.** Having many interrelated facets and being complicated to understand or solve: INTRICATE. "This blatt is too L. to learn without a chavrusa." **2.** Tending to understand everything as a complex process: LOGICAL. "He's too L. just to teach him how to drive without explaining the mechanics involved." [<Yid. <Heb. למד (learn)]

lom-dus (למדות) *n.* **1.** Reason or sound judgment, generally with many interrelated facets or parts: LOGIC. "I have more respect for the subway system now that I chap the L. behind it." **2.** Intricate process: PROCEDURE.

"There's a whole L. to making your own tfillin. You're better off just buying a good pair." **3.** Inventiveness, novelty, or cleverness: INGENUITY. "I thought it was just a poshute nigun until I figured out the L. in the harmonies." [cf. lomdish(e)]

lo-shon (לשון) *n.* **1.** Tone of voice or style of speaking or writing indicative of implicit feeling, character, or the like: DICTION. "His L. made me think he was actually more enthusiastic than he let on." **2.** Parlance of a specialized field: TERMINOLOGY. "The new bochur has gevaltike kishroinos, but it's poshut not shayach for him to hear Rebbe's lomdus in shiur until he can chap the yeshivishe L." [<Heb. לשון (tongue)]

lo-shon sa-gi no-hor (לשון סגי נהור) *n.* A terminology used to replace a terminology that the speaker finds unpleasant or inappropriate: EUPHEMISM. "When the dentist said the area would be 'sensitive,' I think it was L." [<Aram. cf. loshon + סגי (ample) + נהור (shine)]

lu ye-tzu-uyar (לו יצוייר) *conj.* **1.** Used to introduce a clause with the implication "in the event that": (EVEN) IF. "It's so late that, L. I left right now, I'd still miss the chupa." *prep.* **2.** Accepted or supposed to be so without proof or demonstration: ASSUMING. "L. that ois-varf is telling the truth about why he left the last yeshiva, I still wouldn't let him learn here." [<Heb. לו (if) + ציר (engrave)]

M

ma-a-rich (מאריך) *p.a.(t)* **1.** To cause to be longer than necessary: EXTEND. "If you're M. your chabura, the oilam may lose interest." *p.a.(i)* **2.** Characterized by the tendency to say in more time and words than necessary: LONG-WINDED. "I could follow shiur better if Rebbe weren't always M." **3.** To discuss or speak about or to write about at length: TREAT. "The sefer was M. to be sure that no one would use the chidush to pasken from." [<Heb. ארך (length)]

mach-er (מאכער) *n.* An influential, important—or self-important—person: BIGSHOT. "The M. managed to get himself into every picture of the Rosh Yeshiva." [<Yid. <HG machen (make)]

mach-la (מחלה) *n.* **1.** Sickness or illness: DISEASE. "The whole dorm came down with the same M., and almost no one came to shiur." **2.** *(cf.* meshugas) A disreputable practice or fad: CRAZE. "I don't see how the bochrim could get caught up in the M.

of paying hundreds of dollars for sneakers." [<Heb. חלה (ill)]
—**N.B.** Def. 1 may be used euphemistically for specific, particularly grave, diseases.

mach-mir (מחמיר) *p.a.(i)* **1.** Being extremely careful regarding minute details: METICULOUS. "He is always M. to brush his hat and straighten his tie before he goes out in public." **2.** Taking the stricter position on an issue: UNCOMPROMISING. "Even when he travels, he's M. only to eat pas Yisroel and bishel Yisroel." *n.* **3.** One who insists on exactness, stringency, completeness, etc., in the observance of something: STICKLER. "He's a Big M. and occasionally annoys everyone with his extreme practices." [cf. chumra]

mach-ri-a (מכריע) *p.a.(t,i)* **1.** To reach a definite choice after some indecision: SETTLE. "He considered a few yeshivas for his son before he was M. on the one farthest from home." **2.** To make a choice: DECIDE. "I think the

53

hanhalla had been M. before they even heard my suggestion." **3.** To decide with great conviction: RESOLVE. "The bochrim were M. that chaburas should only be held outside of seder." [<Heb. כרע (bow)]

mach-shiv (מחשיב) *p.a.(t)* **1.** To feel or display esteem for: RESPECT. "The more I get to know the older bochrim, the more I'm M. them." **2.** To consider to be important: VALUE. "He is M. his education enough to study hard and do his homework." **3.** To be able to recognize the value or importance of: APPRECIATE. "It takes some experience to be M. the real gadlus of mashgiach's derech in musar." [<Heb. חשב (think)]

ma-doch (מה דאך) *conj.* **1.** In recognition of the relatively obvious situation that: SINCE, IF. "M. I have some money and don't take vacations, he, who is totally broke, should zicher stay home." *prep.* **2.** Take note of the relatively obvious situation of: CONSIDER. "M. my brother. He constantly eats and never gains weight. I should zicher be able to lose weight with a simple diet." [<Yid. <HG doch (yet)]

mad-rei-ga (מדריגה) *n.* **1.** *(followed usually by "in")* Size or quantity: MEASURE. "Eretz Yisroel is the highest M. of kedusha." **2.** A division or grouping of like items within a system: CATEGORY, CLASS. "There are three M. in yeshivishe hats: yeshivish, gor yeshivish, and greasy." **3.** A quan-

tifiable measure within a progression: DEGREE. "There are various M. of chillul Shabbos legabei a sick person." **4.** Grade of quality or excellence: CALIBER. "The yeshiva has a beautiful campus, but the M. of learning there is really low." **5.** A measure of social status: STRATUM. "As a bochur in the yeshiva, there are four M. by which to advance: new bochur, bochur, top guy, and eltere bochur." **6.** An individual point or period in a process or progression: STAGE. "The doctor says that this M. heals in three M." [<Heb. דרג (hill)]

maf-sid (מפסיד) *p.a.(t)* **1.** To use up or spend undesirably: WASTE. "The delay at the border was M. so much time that he just turned around and went home." **2.** To cause the loss or expenditure of: COST. "My membership at the health club was M. me hundreds of dollars since I never used it." [<Heb. פסד (lose)]

ma-ha-lach (מהלך) *n.* **1.** A trip that is perceived to be long and arduous: DISTANCE. "For some people, even a block is too big a M. to go to learn." **2.** The method used in dealing with or accomplishing something: APPROACH. "Even the Menahel had to admit he was impressed with the bochrim's M. for breaking into the kitchen." **3.** The aggregate of methods by which one reflects one's character through one's actions: CONDUCT. "His M. is simple, but he's a deep thinker." [<Heb. הלך (walk)]

ma-hus (מהות) *n.* **1.** The definitive trait or characteristic: CORE, NATURE, ESSENCE. "The M. of the problem is in the fact that it's so complex." **2.** A habitual or characteristic mode of approaching a situation: MANNERISM. "His whole M. is just too weird for me to learn with him all the way through seder." **3.** The particular aim or purpose for which something exists or is designed: FUNCTION, POINT. "The M. of the Beis Medrash is for learning. It just doesn't make a good shul." [<Heb. מה (what)]

mai-la (מעלה) *n.* **1.** Commendable quality or trait: VIRTUE. "The tzaddik was too soft-spoken for most people to realize his M." **2.** Superior position or condition: ADVANTAGE. "Price is the only M. of a discount airline." **3.** An added positive feature or quality: ASSET. "The air bags are the car's greatest M." [<Heb. עלה (rise)]

mai-le or moi-rid (מעלה ומוריד) *p.a.(i)* To have an effect, whether beneficial or detrimental: MATTER. "It's not M. which way the river is flowing if you're trying to cross it." [<Heb. cf. maila + ירד (descend)]

mai-se (מעשה) *n.* **1.** A tale or event related: STORY. "He made up some M. to explain why he never showed up." **2.** A short story or tale related for its significance: ANECDOTE. "I told him a M. from my younger days in Europe to encourage his learning." **3.** Distinct event or occurrence: INCI-

DENT. "I had such a M. the last time I asked him for a favor that I'll never try again." **4.** Set of circumstances: AFFAIR, SITUATION. "The M. is that I can't go with you until later." **5.** A distinct deed: ACT. "He did such a cruel M. that I'm not sure I can forgive him." **6.** An act recognized officially to effect the validity of a transaction, a legal circumstance, and the like: ENACTMENT. "It's not enough just to pay the money if you don't make a M. to show the kinyan." [<Heb. עשה (do)]

make a wash Cf. wash.

ma-kir (מכיר) *p.a.(i)* **1.** To grasp or understand fully or clearly: REALIZE. "Until you hear him say shiur, you can't be M. how smart he is." **2.** To apprehend the value of: APPRECIATE. "I can tell by how you talk about him that you're not M. the favor he did for you." [<Heb. נכר (strange)]

ma-kom (מקום) *n., pl.* **mekoimos 1.** A place or locality: LOCATION. "This is not a good M. to keep your radio. The Mashgiach will find it in a minute." **2.** Societal status: POSITION, PLACE. "That little kid who tried to give me musar had better learn his M." **3.** Rational basis: GROUNDS. "You were caught, and you have no M. to complain about the knas." [<Heb. קום (stance)] **Cf.** sakana.

mak-pid (מקפיד) *p.a.(i)* **1.** To be resolute on some matter involving particular attention: INSIST. "He is M. on buying the best material for his clothes." **2.** To abstain or refrain from participating or partaking: PASS. "The yeshiva is M. on accepting money from people who are not Shomer Shabbos." **3.** To disallow or decry: FROWN. "Rebbe is M. on any talking during shiur." **4.** To request or call for with authority: DEMAND. "Rebbe is M. that there be no talking during shiur." **5.** To be concerned, to take responsibility: CAREFUL. "You should be M. to keep your room clean. You never know when your parents may show up." [<Heb. קפד (shield)]

ma-mash (ממש) *adv.* **1.** As though true to fact: LITERALLY. "My chavrusa M. tore my svara to pieces." **2.** Surely or certainly: DEFINITELY. "Are you M. leaving right now, or can I get a package to send with you?" **3.** Actually, genuinely, indeed: REALLY. "I ate the whole cake, and I M. enjoyed it." **4.** To a high degree: VERY. "The prices in the new store are M. cheap." *interj.* **5.** Enthusiastic response: WOW. "M! I can't believe anyone could survive a crash like that." [<Heb. ממש (substance)]

ma-mash-us (ממשות) *n.* Real worth, value, or effect: SUBSTANCE. "He made a feeble excuse, but it had no M. to it." [cf. mamash]

mam-shich (ממשיך) *p.a.(t,i)* To continue after some interruption: RESUME. "I have to run now, but we can

be M. this conversation later." [<Heb. משך (pull)]

mar-beh (מרבה) *p.a.(t)* To imply or to express in a manner as to incorporate that which may not be obvious: INCLUDE, COVER. "I said I wanted fleishig to be M. chicken." [<Heb. רב (great)]

ma she-ein kein (מה שאין כן) *prep. & conj.* On the other hand; in contrast to: UNLIKE. "I have experience and education, M. him. That's why they gave me the job instead of him." [<Heb. מה (what) + שאין (that is not) + כן (thus)]

mash-gi-ach (משגיח) *n., pl.* **mashgichim 1.** A counselor and spiritual advisor in a yeshiva: GUIDE. "Our M. helps us by giving us advice." **2.** Bossy, unsolicited advisor: CONSCIENCE. "My roommate acts like my M., constantly telling me what to do." **3.** Overseer or inspector: SUPERVISOR. "The M. had the job of checking the kashrus of the meat." [<Heb. שגח (view)]

mash-lim (משלים) *p.a.(t)* **1.** To compensate for that which is missing: MAKE UP. "I was away for two days, so I have to be M. the Daf Yomi." **2.** To supply that which is deficient or desired: FILL IN. "The building will be beautiful when they are M. all the details." [<Heb. שלם (whole)]

mash-ma (משמע) *p.a.(i)* **1.** Cognizable, easy to perceive: EVIDENT. "It's M. from the story that the criminal was never caught." *p.a.(t)* **2.** To hint without saying openly or directly: IMPLY. "The Gemara is M. that the Earth is round." **3.** To make known, give a sign, indicate: INTIMATE. "He was M. that he would leave right away, but you can check for his car." [<Heb. שמע (hear)]

mash-pi-a (משפיע) *usually followed by "on," p.a.(t)* **1.** To have an effect on the nature or behavior of: INFLU-ENCE. "The musar talks were M. on him to deal with his peers better." **2.** To produce and impress an effect: AFFECT. "The weather was M. on the day's schedule of events." **3.** To cause to act or think undesirably: SWAY. "I think that new bochur was M. on everyone to start talking during class." **4.** To cause to act or think desirably: IM-PRESS. "The older bochur was M. on my brother to learn more." [<Heb.שפע (abound)]

ma-sig (משיג) *p.a.(t)* **1.** To take the time to conceive of: UNDERSTAND. "Until you're older, you'll never be M. how much your Rebbeim have done for you." **2.** To be able to imagine: FATHOM. "Americans just can't be M. the kind of corruption and poverty they have in Third World countries." [<Heb. שוג (type)]

mas-ka-na (מסקנה) *n.* Outcome, final analysis: UPSHOT. "The M. of the Mashgiach's talk with me is that I'd better behave until the end of the zman." [<Aram. נסק (rise)] **Cf.** lemaskana.

mas-kim (מסכים) *p.a.(t&i)* **1.** Favor-ably inclined: WILLING. "If you're M. to help me, we could finish before mincha." **2.** To acknowledge as true, just, or proper: CONCUR. "Everyone is M. that he has kishroinos, but no one can decide how he should use his po-tential." **3.** To grant permission: CON-SENT. "I can't leave town overnight unless the Mashgiach is M." **4.** Finally, to reach an agreement: CONCEDE. "After we argued for a while, my chavrusa was M. that I was right." [<Heb. סכם (total)]

mas-mid (מתמיד) *n., pl.* **masmidim** An assiduous, persevering learner of Torah: DEVOTEE. "The M. sat in Beis Medrash until the Rosh Yeshiva insisted that he go to sleep." [<Yid. <emulative of Heb. תמיד (always)]

ma-tir (מתיר) *vt., or occasionally p.a.(t)* To allow or permit: SANC-TION. "Since the bochrim needed to pack for Bein HaZmanim, the Mashgiach M. keeping the lights on past midnight." [<Heb. נתר (jump)]

mat-ri-ach (מטריח) *p.a.(t)* To cause to expend effort, or to cause annoyance: BOTHER. "If I didn't have back trouble, I wouldn't be M. you to help me." [<Heb. טרח (effort)] **Cf.** tircha.

ma-tzav (מצב) *n., pl.* **matzavim 1.** State of affairs: CIRCUMSTANCE. "I slipped on the ice and into the inter-section and found myself in a bad M." **2.** Financial situation: CIRCUM-

STANCES. "I can't lend you any money now; my business is in a bad M." **3.** Situation with respect to circumstances: CONDITION. "If you think it looks bad now, you should have seen the M. of the car right after the accident." [<Heb. נצב (stand)] —**N.B.** Matzav is a singular noun despite the translation for def. 2.

matz-li-ach (מצליח) *p.a.(i)* **1.** To thrive: PROSPER. "As soon as he began to be M. in his business, the yeshiva sent someone to him to collect." **2.** Accomplishing a mission or an attempt: SUCCESSFUL. "They were M. in collecting enough money to start the new building." [<Heb.צלח (aim)] **Cf.** hatzlocha.

maz-bir (מסביר) *p.a.(t&i)* To render clear or understandable: EXPLAIN. "Please be M. why you were looking through my things." [<Heb. סבר (consider)]

ma-zel (מזל) *n.* Chance or good fortune: LUCK. "Sometimes success comes more from M. than from talent." [<Heb. נזל (flow)]

ma-zik (מזיק) *p.a.(t)* **1.** To ruin partially: DAMAGE. "Anyone who is M. any part of the yeshiva gets a knas." **2.** To be the source of some detriment to: HURT. "I have to protect my interests, and if he's M. me, I'll take him to a Din Torah." *n., pl.* **mazikim 3.** A malicious, ruthless person: CUT-THROAT. "He's a big M., and I advise you not to do any business with him." **4.** One who enjoys causing problems: TROUBLEMAKER. "He wanted to get involved in the argument because he's a M. by nature." **5.** A rambunctious, wild person: MENACE. "That kid who slept over was such a M. that we had to clean up for two days." [<Heb. נזק (damage)]

me-a-kev (מעכב) *p.a.(i)* **1.** Required for some purpose: REQUISITE, NECESSARY. "It's M. to have permission before you leave the yeshiva's property." *p.a.(t)* **2.** To delay and prevent: HINDER. "The way the guy next to me was parked was M. from getting my car out." *n.* **3.** A necessary condition: PREREQUISITE. "Being a native-born citizen is a M. to becoming president." **4.** That which holds back and delays: HINDRANCE, OBSTACLE. "Right now, the only M. to finishing the building is raising the money." [<Heb.עכב (curve)] **Var. for defs. 3 and 4** ikuv.

me-a-yen (מעיין) *usually followed by "in," p.a.(i)* **1.** To skim through by reading random passages: BROWSE. "While I was waiting at the store, I was M. in dozens of seforim." **2.** To engage in research: INVESTIGATE. "I've been M. in dozens of seforim and can't find any way to justify what you're doing." **3.** To examine closely for details: SCRUTINIZE. "I was M. in their faces to try to see what they were thinking." [<Heb. עין (eye)]

me-cha-bed (מכבד) *p.a.(t)* **1.** To hold in high esteem: VENERATE. "Even if no one told you to, you would be M. the Rosh Yeshiva for his gadlus." **2.** To treat with honor: RESPECT. "If you want to stay out of trouble, make sure to be M. everyone in the hanhalla." **3.** To confer an honorary privilege upon: HONOR. "The yeshiva was M. the rich man with an aliya." **4.** To offer or present, particularly in a friendly, informal setting: FURNISH. "While we're waiting for the other guests, let me be M. you with some cake and coffee." [<Heb. כבד (weight)]

me-cha-desh (מחדש) *p.a.(i)* **1.** To bring into being or activity: DEVELOP. "Newton was M. calculus." **2.** To make known or available: INTRODUCE, ADD. "The new math teacher was M. calculus as part of the curriculum." *p.a.(t)* **3.** To add a new element as part of a composite: CONTRIBUTE. "I can't see what mailos calculus has been M." [<Heb. חדש (new)]

me-cha-lek (מחלק) *p.a.(i)* **1.** To perceive a difference: DISTINGUISH. "It's not always easy to be M. between din and minhag." **2.** To impose dissimilarities on putatively like items: DIFFERENTIATE. "You can be M. between the twins by looking in their eyes." [<Heb. חלק (part)]

me-cha-ven (מכוון) *usually followed by "in" p.a.(i)* **1.** To find oneself in inadvertent accord with: CONCUR. "Before I knew that he had said it in shiur, I was M. to the Rosh Yeshiva's pshat in the Gemara." **2.** To refer to without citing: ALLUDE. "Although he was afraid to say so publicly, he was M. in his speech to a Zohar." **3.** To perform willfully and with forethought: INTEND. "When I saw him running at me, I was sure he was M. to hurt me." [<Heb. כן (set)]

me-cha-yeh (מחיה) *n.* That which provides satisfaction: PLEASURE, INDULGENCE. "It was such a M. to have a chance to swim when the weather was so hot." [<Yid. <Heb. חי (live)]

me-cha-yev (מחייב) *p.a.(t)* **1.** To induce by power or by means of authority: FORCE. "The Rosh Yeshiva was M. him to eat supper to keep his strength up." **2.** To elicit a response by appeal to a sense of obligation: COMPEL. "His feeling of gratitude was M. him to call his grandparents every week." [<Heb. חוב (oblige)]

me-cha-zek (מחזק) *p.a.(t)* To strengthen spiritually or emotionally: ENCOURAGE. "He was depressed that his learning was so weak, but the Mashgiach took the time to be M. him." [<Heb. חזק (strong)]

me-chi-la (מחילה) *n.* **1.** The granting of absolution or pardon: FORGIVENESS. "I tried to explain my mistake, but he wouldn't give me M. for it." *in* *the phrase, "ask mechila," vi.* To request forgiveness: APOLOGIZE. "If you think you were wrong, you should ask M." [cf. moichel]

me-chu-bad-ik(e) *adj.* **1.** Having distinction and honor: REGARDED. "To be the Mashgiach is to have one of the most M. positions in the yeshiva." **2.** Appreciable in size, number, or amount: RESPECTABLE. "Corporate lawyers usually get more M. salaries than Rebbeim do." [cf. mechabed] **Var.** bekavodik(e), bekavod.

me-chu-tzaf (מחוצף) *n.* One who behaves impudently: SMART ALECK. "That M. insulted his parents, his Rebbeim, and me." [cf. chutzpa]

me-chu-yav (מחוייב) *adj. (p.a. only)* **1.** Compelled by law, promise, or the like: OBLIGED. "A citizen is M. to register with the draft." **2.** Liable to be called upon to answer for: RESPONSIBLE. "The Menahel is M. to provide a financial statement of the yeshiva to the major donors." **3.** Morally or ethically motivated: DUTY BOUND. "He felt he was M. to volunteer to help his Rebbe build a Sukkah." **4.** Owing money: INDEBTED. "I can't look him in the eye until I'm no longer M. so much money to him." **5.** *Var of* chayav. [cf. mechayev]

me-dak-dek (מדקדק) *p.a.(i)* **1.** Thorough or painstaking; avoiding error by virtue of the care exercised: CAREFUL. "He was M. about his manners at his meeting with the Rosh Yeshiva." **2.** Extremely careful based on an ethical, logical, moral, or other standard: SCRUPULOUS. "He is M. to hear all the sides before reaching a decision." **3.** Concerned in a finicky manner based on the fear of error: METICULOUS. "He is M. to wear the latest styles in public." **4.** Having an exaggerated regard for the fine points of the rules and forms prescribed by law or custom: PUNCTILIOUS. "He is very M. to be exactly on time for davening, never early or late." *n.* **5.** A person guided by a personal standard or attitude demanding perfection: PERFECTIONIST. "The teacher is a big M. and fails you for even one point." **6.** A philologist or specialist in language: GRAMMARIAN. "He is enough of a M. to help you learn up the Ibn Ezra." [<Heb. דק (sharp)] **Var. for def. 6** baal dikduk.

me-da-meh (מדמה) *p.a.(t)* To draw an analogy: COMPARE. "You can't be M. learning Gemara to learning math." [cf. dimyon]

me-da-yek (מדייק) *occasionally followed by "in," p.a.(i)* **1.** To infer a conclusion or interpretation based on careful attention to diction: DEDUCE. "We were M. from the announcement that we would have school despite the snow." **2.** To exact a true meaning in a statement or situation by careful examination: PROBE. "If you're M., you'll see that the speaker is actually very nervous." [<Heb. דק (sharp)]

me-far-sem (מפרסם) *p.a.(t)* **1.** To make known that which is secret or hidden: REVEAL. "I hope the teacher isn't M. my grade to everyone." **2.** To make more widely known that which is known only to some: PUBLICIZE. "The radio was M. the school closings." [<Aram. פרסם <Heb. פרץ (spread)]

me-fu-nak (מפונק) *adj. (p.a. only)* **1.** Being particularly concerned about cleanliness, appearance, and the way things are prepared: FINICKY, SPOILED. "It doesn't pay to be so M. if you have to live in a dorm." *n. pl.* **mefunakim 2.** One who is particularly concerned about cleanliness, appearance, and the way things are prepared: FUSSBUDGET. "He's such a M. that all the caterers know him from his constant complaints about the food at chassunas." [<Aram. פנק (freeman)]

me-ga-rei-a (מגרע) *p.a.(i)* **1.** To take away or worsen: DETRACT. "Skipping over the Aggadeta is M. from what is otherwise a great shiur."*p.a.(t)* **2.** To reduce in effectiveness or intensity: WEAKEN. "The inability to maintain active youth is M. the credibility of alternative Jewish organizations." [<Heb. גרע (withdraw)]

me-ha-neh (מהנה) *p.a.(t)* To give satisfaction, pleasure, joy, etc.: PLEASE. "I only work at my grades to be M. my parents." [cf. hanaa]

me-hei-cha tei-si (מהיכא תיתי) *Interrogative conj.* Expresses that a previ-

ous clause may be predicated upon a faulty premise: WHO SAYS. "I'll help you look, but M. you dropped your wallet near here?" [<Aram. מהיכא (whence) + תיתי (come)]

me-id (מעיד) *p.a.(t)* To testify or provide testimony to: ATTEST. "I can be M. that the hanhalla is cracking down on curfew. The Mashgiach caught me twice this week." [<Heb. עד (witness)]

mei-kl (מקיל) *p.a.(i)* **1.** Not harsh or strict: EASYGOING. "The bochrim only like that teacher because he is M. in marking tests." **2.** Yielding to wishes: INDULGENT. "The Mashgiach is never M. on attendance at seder." **3.** Taking the lenient position: LIBERAL. "The Beis Din was M. on the damages, and only awarded a few dollars." *n., pl.* **mekilim 4.** One who is not strict: LIBERAL, LATITUDINARIAN. "He went there specifically with his shaila, because that Rabbi is known to be a M." [<Heb. קל (light)]

mei-la (מילא) *interj.* **1.** Expression of disinterest or that a premise is irrelevant: SO WHAT. "M. My roommate's complaints won't stop me from listening to my tapes." *conj.* **2.** Indication that a premise was innocuous: WHEN. "M. he wanted me to learn with him for an hour, I was maskim. Now he thinks I'm going to stay with him all day; he can forget it." [cf. mimeila]

mei-vin (מבין) *n., pl.* **mevinim** An expert or proficient person: CON-

NOISSEUR. "I'm not such a M.; just give me a bottle of simple wine." [<Heb. בון (understand)]

me-ka-bel (מקבל) *p.a.(t)* **1.** To take into one's possession that which has been sent or given: RECEIVE. "The chassan wasn't used to being M. so many gifts." **2.** To promise, agree, or obligate oneself to perform: UNDER-TAKE. "The bochur was M. to learn one hundred blatt during the zman." **3.** To accept credibility or truth of: BELIEVE. "I couldn't be M. that he learned so many blatt in just one zman." *p.a.(i)* **4.** To accept or believe to be credible: BUY IT. "It's not that I don't understand your story; I'm just not M." [<Heb. קבל (receive)]

me-kan-ne (מקנא) *p.a.(t)* To be jealous of qualities in another: ENVY. "I'm only M. him because he's smart." [<Heb. קנא (vengeance)]

me-ka-rev (מקרב) *p.a.(t)* **1.** To welcome and treat amicably: BEFRIEND. "I'm thankful to that family for having been M. me when I was away from home." **2.** To introduce irreligious Jews to the rules and principles of Orthodoxy: INDOCTRINATE. "He was M. his neighbors to the point that they began to eat exclusively kosher food." [<Heb. קרב (near)] —N.B. *Nominal form for def. 2* kiruv: INDOCTRINATION.

me-ka-tzer (מקצר) *p.a.(t)* **1.** To decrease the size, length, duration, etc., of: SHORTEN. "The yeshiva was M. the zman to let the bochrim go to summer camp." *p.a.(i)* **2.** To treat only briefly: CONCISE. "Although the sefer is very M., its message is powerful." [<Heb. קצר (short)]

me-kor (מקור) *n., pl.* **mekoros 1.** Grounds for an unusual or innovative statement or argument: BASIS. "The M. for his chidush is in the Medrash." **2.** A passage mentioned: CITATION. "Where is the M. for the Gemara Rebbe spoke out in shiur?" **3.** The source from which something is derived: ORIGIN. "Where can I find the M. for the minhagim of Hoshana Rabba?" [<Heb. קרר (bore)]

me-lo-cha (מלאכה) *n.* **1.** That which requires exertion or effort: TASK. "The bochrim gave up trying to plan a chassan party when it became too big a M. for them." **2.** Art or skill: TRADE. "He's not a simple electrician; he knows the M. really well." [<Heb. מלאכה (work)]

me-ma-yet (ממעט) *p.a.(t)* To indicate the exclusion of: PRECLUDE. "I specifically said to eat fruit to be M. junk food." [cf. miyut]

mentsh (מענטש) *n., pl.* **mentshen** An honest, decent person: HUMAN BEING. "He's a real M. to offer to learn with the slower bochrim." [<Yid. <HG Mensch (person)]

me-nu-val (מנוול) *Var. of* mushchas.

me-o-rer (מעורר) *p.a.(t)* **1.** To note or point out: MENTION. "Only one bochur was M. that the teacher had forgotten about the test." **2.** To stimulate into action: MOTIVATE. "Rebbe was M. everyone to go out and help the teacher push his car off the ice." **3.** To rekindle, as in a memory or the like: TRIGGER. "Just the smell of the yeshiva kitchen is M. the worst memories of living in the dorm." [<Heb. ער (awake)]

merk uhn (אנמערקען) *vt.* To remark, note, or draw attention to: POINT OUT. "The pessimist always M. the chisroinos of all our plans." [<Yid. <HG merken (mark, note)]

me-sa-der (מסדר) *p.a.(t)* To place in an order or succession: ARRANGE. "He was M. his shiur notes into one organized folder." [cf. seder]

me-sa-ken (מתקן) *p.a.(t)* **1.** To declare and establish as a rule: INSTITUTE. "Rebbe was M. that everyone has to learn two halachos every day." **2.** To decide and put into effect: FIX. "The Menahel was M. the hours for locking the doors to the buildings." **3.** To restore to a good condition: REPAIR. "I've been M. my watch band temporarily, but I have to get to a jeweler." [<Heb. תקן (fix)]

me-sa-lek (מסלק) *p.a.(t)* **1.** To clear away: REMOVE. "He didn't actually help me advance, but he was M. some obstacles." **2.** To relinquish associa-

tion with: EXCLUDE. "To avoid taking sides, he was M. himself from the argument." [<Heb. סלק (depart)]

me-sha-bed (משעבד) *p.a.(t)* To cause to be obligated: COMMIT. "I plan to go, but I can't be M. myself to the time." [<Aram. <Heb. עבד (work)]

me-sha-dech (משדך) *p.a.(t)* To arrange a meeting: INTRODUCE. "Once he was M. me to the computer, I could never use a typewriter again." [cf. shiduch]

me-shu-bad (משועבד) *adj. (p.a. only)* **1.** Required or responsible: OBLIGATED. "Since I had promised, I was M. to help him with the Mishna." **2.** Indebted or bound: BEHOLDEN. "He's helped me in the past, so I was M. to help him when he asked." **3.** At the mercy of: TIED. "I want to take my car, so I'm not M. to someone else's schedule." [cf. meshabed]

me-shu-ga (משוגע) *adj. (p.a. only)* Irrational or crazy: INSANE. "It's M. to drive so fast at night in the mountains." [<Heb. שגע (insane)]
—**N.B.** preceding a noun: meshugana.

me-shu-ga-na (משוגענער) *n.* **1.** A crazy person: NUT. "He's a M. He went to Florida just to get fresher orange juice." *adj.* **2.** Cf. meshuga. [cf. meshuga]

me-shu-gas (משוגעת) *n., pl.* **meshugasen 1.** A distinctly strange or absurd act or practice: ECCENTRICITY, QUIRK. "It's just a M. he has to wear only green ties." **2.** A preoccupation leading to oddities of behaviors: HANG-UP. "My roommate has a M. about cleanliness, and he's always accusing me of messing things up." **3.** Foolishness, absurdity, or insanity: NONSENSE. "Cut out the M., and get to work." [cf. meshuga] **Var.** shtik.

me-shu-ne (משונה) *adj. (p.a. only)* Irregular or aberrant: WEIRD. "It's M. that none of the bochrim showed up for dinner." [<Heb. שנה (change)]

me-shu-ne-dik (משונה-דיק) *adv.* **1.** Markedly out of the ordinary: UNUSUALLY. "The Baal Tefilla has a M. wonderful voice." **2.** Noteworthy for excellence: INCREDIBLY. "I was in tears because the badchan was so M. funny." [cf. meshune]

me-shu-ne-dik(e) (משונה-דיק) *adj.* Markedly odd or irregular: BIZARRE. "The speaker had some M. ideas that caused us not to trust him." [cf. meshune]

me-su-dar (מסודר) *adj. (p.a. only)* Placed in an order or succession: ORGANIZED. "He was always prepared since he was so M." [cf. seder] **Var. and preceding a noun,** mesudardike.

me-su-dar-dik(e) Cf. mesudar.

me-su-pak (מסופק) *(adj. p.a. only)* Having doubts about: UNCERTAIN.

"I'm still M. about whether the yeshiva will accept my son. That's why I'm looking at other places." [cf. sofek] **Var.** besofek.

me-tzi-us (מציאות) *n.* **1.** That which has occurred: THE FACTS. "I don't want to hear your commentary; just tell me the M." **2.** Set of circumstances: SITUATION. "You can't ask a kashe on a maise since the M. in the maise may have been completely different." **3.** That which is actual: FACT. "Your kashe has no shaichus to the M. of this inyan." **4.** An irrefutable statement: FACT. "It's just M. that water flows downhill." [<Heb. מצא (find)]

me-vat-tel (מבטל) *Var. of* battel.

me-va-yesh (מבייש) *p.a.(t)* To cause shame to: EMBARRASS. "When he told everyone my bad grade, the teacher was M. me publicly." [<Heb. בוש (embarrass)] **Var.** boosh out.

me-va-zeh (מבזה) *p.a.(t)* **1.** To hold in contempt: SCORN. "You shouldn't be M. him just because you don't get along with him." **2.** To display contempt for: HUMILIATE. "I didn't want to be M. my chavrusa, so I never told him how bad I thought his pshat was." [<Heb. בזה (despise)]

me-ya-ches (מייחס) *p.a.(t)* To accredit or attribute: ASCRIBE. "If you say over someone else's pshat, be sure to be M. it to him." [<Heb. יחס (relate)]

me-ya-yesh (מייאש) *p.a.(i)* To give up hope: DESPAIR. "I was M. from finding someone who could explain this Tosfos to me." [<Heb. יאש (resigned)] —**N.B.** Often refers specifically to despair of finding that which has been lost.

me-za-rez (מזרז) *p.a.(t)* To urge or spur into action: STIR. "I even offered my son money to be M. him to learn better." [cf. zrizus]

mi-da (מידה) *n., generally pl.* **midos** **1.** Behavior, attitude, etc., distinguishing one's personality or nature: TRAIT. "Some people only survive if they have a M. of cruelty and can watch others suffer." **2.** Moral or admirable virtue: QUALITY. "He's lazy, but his M. of honesty makes him a good employee." [<Heb. מדד (measure)]

mi-dos Cf. mida.

mi-mei-la (ממילא) *adv.* **1.** Occurring without initiative as a consequence: AUTOMATICALLY. "Learn in the right yeshiva, and M. you'll get a better shiduch." **2.** Resultantly or as a consequence: THEREFORE. "I never asked him mechila. M. he's still mad." [<Aram. (of itself)]

mi-muh nif-shach (ממה נפשך) *adv.* **1.** In consideration that all sides are equal: EITHER WAY. "I can go by plane or train. It will be expensive M." **2.** Without consideration of alterna-

tives: REGARDLESS, ANYWAY. "I can give you a ride; I'm going M." [<Aram. ממה (from what) + נפשך (yourself)]

mi-nei u-bei (מיניה וביה) *adv.* As an integral component: INTRINSICALLY. "I can't answer your shaila, because it is M. based on a mistake." [<Aram. מיניה (of it) + וביה (and in it)]

mi-she-bei-rach (מי שבירך) *Var. of* parsha, def. 3.

mish-ta-tef (משתתף) *p.a.(i)* **1.** To become involved: JOIN. "I've been M. in a chabura, but I've never said one." **Usually followed by "in" 2.** To help out toward a common goal: CHIP IN FOR. "I was M. in the party, but I didn't go." [Heb. שתף (connect)]

mis-po-yel (מתפעל) *p.a.(i)* **1.** To stand in awe: MARVEL. "I was M. by the power of Niagara Falls." **2.** Deeply affected in opinion, feelings, or emotion: IMPRESSED. "I'm not M. by the shoddy new building the yeshiva put up." [<Heb. פעל (activity)] **Var.** nispoyel, chap hispailus.

mis-ta-ber (מסתבר) *adj. (p.a. only)* **1.** Probably destined: LIKELY. "It's not M. that the yeshiva raised more money than it spent last year." **2.** Within the parameters of logic or sound judgments: REASONABLE. "It's M. to say that the bochrim didn't love the supper even though they ate it." [cf. svara]

mis-ta-ma (מסתמא) *adv.* **1.** Barring any difficulty: PROBABLY. "He's M. got enough money to take a short trip; he's been working a while." **2.** Based on a best guess: PRESUMABLY. "M. you can ask him pshat. He learned it last zman." [<Aram. <Heb. סתם (plain)]

mit-a-muhl (מיטאמאל) *adv.* Suddenly; without warning: UNEXPECTEDLY. "He was doing well in yeshiva out of town, and M. he felt he needed to live at home." [<Yid. <HG mit (with) + einmal (once)]

mi-tzad (מצד) *prep.* In consideration of the needs or demands of: AS TO. "M. me we can leave now, but we have to wait for the other passengers to be ready." [cf. tzad]

mitz-va (מצוה) *n.* **1.** An obligatory precept or observance: REQUIRE-MENT. "He goes to visit the hospitals just to do the M." **2.** An act of kindness: FAVOR. "Do a M. and help that little boy tie his shoes." **3.** An act deemed praiseworthy or within the spirit of the law: EXPECTATION. "There's a M. to clean the house for Shabbos." [<Heb. צוה (command)] —**N.B.** The phrase "a mitzva" as a predicate nominative may be more naturally translated: LAUDABLE or EXPECTED.

mi-yus (מיאוס) *adj.* Disgusting in nature: REPULSIVE. "Dinner in yeshiva was M., so I had to go for pizza." [<Heb. מאס (abhor)] **Var.** mous, miyusdik(e).

mi-yus-dik(e) (מיאוס-דיק) *Var. of* miyus.

mi-yut (מיעוט) *n., pl.* **miyutim** The smaller number: MINORITY. "Only the M. of bochrim who can stand it look forward to lunch in yeshiva." [<Heb. מעט (few)]

mo-dern *adj.* Characterized by a per-ceived lack of rigor or strict attention to more than the absolutely requisite Orthodox values or practices: LIB-ERAL. "His views are too M. for the principal to let him teach in the elementary school." [<Eng.] **Var.** modernish(e).

modernish(e) *Var. of* modern.

mod-ne (מאדנע) *adj.* Unpleasantly unusual or clumsy: ODD. "His behav-ior was so M. that the Mashgiach rec-ommended professional help." [<Yid. <HG Mode (style, fashion)]

moi-chel (מוחל) *p.a.(t)* **1.** To excuse or pardon: FORGIVE. "I'm M. you even though you embarrassed me in pub-lic." **2.** To give up all claim to or ac-count of: FORGO. "I'm broke now. Please be M. the money I owe you." **Usually followed by "on" 3.** To relin-quish intentionally: WAIVE. "The teacher is M. his kavod and lets the bochrim walk all over him." *p.a.(i)* **4.** Ceasing to bear resentment for: OVER

IT. "Stop apologizing already; I'm M." [<Heb. מחל (excuse)]

moi-chi-ach (מוכיח) *p.a.(t)* **1.** To prove, set in motion, and/or verify the validity of: ESTABLISH. "Some countries use history to be M. that they have a right to their claims." **2.** To establish the truth or verity of by evidence or proof: DEMONSTRATE. "If you can be M. that there is a real need, the oilam will contribute to your cause." **3.** To criticize mildly or even amicably with the intention to correct a fault or pattern of misbehavior: REPROVE. "The Mashgiach was M. him privately for taking naps during seder." [cf. koyach]

moi-de (מודה) *p.a.(t)* **1.** To admit something embarrassing or awkward, usually under duress: ACKNOWLEDGE, COME CLEAN. "The bochur was M. that he was hiding a TV in his room." **2.** To acknowledge boldly an implication formerly denied or equivocated: CONFESS. "Once the yeshiva had found out, the bochur was M. that he was attending college at night." **3.** To admit due to overwhelming evidence: CONCEDE. "Seeing the results, he had to be M. that he was guilty of bad judgment." [<Heb. הדה (admit)]

moi-di-a (מודיע) *p.a.(t)* **1.** To make known to: INFORM. "The principal was M. the oilam that school would close because of snow." **2.** To present as public knowledge: ANNOUNCE. "The Menahel was M. the names of

the bochrim who needed to go for farhers." [<Heb. ידע (know)]

moi-nei-a (מונע) *p.a.(t)* **1.** To prevent the agent of an action: KEEP. "The road construction was M. him from getting to the chupah on time." **2.** To conceal or keep secret: WITHHOLD. "The bochrim were mad that the hanhalla was M. information about the schedule for the zman." **3.** To delay by imposing an impediment: HINDER. "The broken oven was M. the cook from having supper ready in time for the bochrim to come from seder." **4.** To prevent the occurrence of the result of an action: OBVIATE, PRECLUDE. "The new yeshiva policy should be M. the possibility of bochrim losing their laundry." **5.** To detract from or lessen: DIMINISH. "Let the Rosh Yeshiva be mesader kidushin in order not to be M. his kavod." [<Heb. מנע (prevent)]

moi-ra-dik(e) (מורא-דיק) *adj.* Of extremely high and impressive quality: TREMENDOUS. "I saw a M. picture of Niagara Falls. You can practically hear the water." [<Heb. ירא (fear)]

moi-ser (מוסר) *n., pl.* **mosrim** A snitch; one who provides potentially injurious information to the authorities: INFORMANT. "If I catch the M. who told the principal I cut class, I'll tear him apart." [<Heb. מסר (transmit)]

moi-sif (מוסיף) *p.a.(i)* **1.** To make clearer by adding information: ELABOR-

ATE. "When the Mashgiach saw that the bochrim were going back to their same practices, he was M. on his rules." **2.** To enhance or increase in quality or beauty: IMPROVE. "The yeshiva thought they could be M. on the appearance of the Beis Medrash just by painting." *p.a.(t&i)* **3.** To contribute toward a completed, final state: ADD. "The music was M. on the atmosphere of the event." [<Heb. יסף (add)]

mo-us (מאוס) *Var. of* miyus.

mu-chach *Var. of* mukach.

much-rach (מוכרח) *adj. (p.a. only)* Unequivocally conveying particular meaning or implication: UNMISTAKABLE. "The yeshiva hasn't raised money in a year; it's M. that they will have to close soon." [<Heb. כרח (force)]

mu-kach (מוכח) *adj. (p.a. only)* Established unequivocally: PLAIN. "It's M. from the color that the water is impure." [cf. koyach] **Var.** muchach.

mun (מאנען) *vt.* **1.** To hold accountable for: REPRIMAND. "The Mashgiach M. him for coming late to seder, and he demanded an explanation." **2.** To claim as a right: DEMAND. "I would rather pay him back before he has a chance to M. the $5.00 from me." **3.** To demand repayment from: CHASE. "I would rather pay him back before he has a chance to M. me for the $5.00." [<Yid. <HG mahnen (remind)] **Var.** *p.a.(t)* toveia.

mu-sag (מושג) *n., pl.* **musagim** **1.** Intuitive understanding: APPREHENSION. "He never pays attention and has no M. of what's going on around him." **2.** General knowledge of a subject: CONCEPT. "He got a tutor because he didn't understand the M. they were working on in class." [cf. masig]

mu-sar (מוסר) *n.* **1.** A useful bit of practical wisdom: A LESSON. "He took M. from his accident and now always wears a seatbelt." **2.** Information of a need for care or attention: A WARNING. "The doctor gave him M. about all the fried food he ate." **3.** A stern expression of disapproval: A HARANGUE. "The cook gave me M. for taking doubles before others had had any." **4.** The study of ethical works intended to improve one's moral conduct: DISCIPLINE. "He's so wild and loud now; imagine what he'd be like if he never learned M." **5. musar out** To reprove sternly: BERATE, LET ONE HAVE IT. "My chavrusa really M. me out for leaving in the middle of seder." [<Heb. יסר (afflict)]

mush-chas (מושחת) *n., pl.* **mushchussim** A coarse, lewd individual: LOWLIFE. "He's such a M. that I'd save a snake's life before his." [<Heb. שחת (depth)] **Var.** menuval.

mu-shel (משל) *n., pl.* **meshullim** **1.** An instance used to illustrate a general circumstance: EXAMPLE. "He explained aviation with a M. of a helicopter." **2.** A partial similarity on which a comparison can be based: ANALOGY. "He explained aviation with a M. of a bird." [<Heb. משל (control, rule)]

mush-lam (מושלם) *n.* One whose good qualities have been developed laboriously and are worthy of emulation: PARAGON. "The Rav is such a M. that people observe his every move, hoping to learn how to improve themselves." [cf. mashlim]

mu-tar (מותר) *adj. (p.a. only)* **1.** Allowed, as in an act potentially within the limitations of a particular law: OK.

"Some hold it's M. to drink coffee before kiddush." **2.** Permitted by law; lawful: LEGAL. "It's M. to turn right on red here." **3.** Allowable and unfettered by possible limitations: UNRESTRICTED. "Many poskim hold that chess is M." [cf. matir]

muz zain (מוזט זיין) *conj.* Of necessity that: NO DOUBT. "I see that your bags are packed; M. you have a ride and permission from the Mashgiach." [<Yid. <HG muss (must) + sein (be)]

N

naf-ka mi-na (נפקא מינה) *n.* **1.** Result of an action or situation: RAMIFICATION. "There is no N. whether I leave now or later; I won't have a ride until tomorrow." **2.** Importance to an individual or to society: RELEVANCY. "What's the N. who's in the World Series? I'm only interested in my learning." **3.** That which distinguishes among like items: DIFFERENCE, DISTINCTION. "I still can't taste the N. between Coke and Pepsi." *conj.* **4.** Introduces that a rhetorical clause bears no relevance to practicality: SO WHAT. "N. if you know all the halachos. That's no ptur for me to stop learning." [<Aram. נפק (exit) + מינה (from it)]

na-ni-ach (נניח) *conj.* Allowing or accepting: ASSUMING, SUPPOSE THAT. "N. your right in lomdus. I'd still be afraid to pasken like that." [cf. hanacha]

na-vi (נביא) *n., pl.* **neviyim** One who seems to have powers of precognition: PSYCHIC. "You must be a N. to know that I only drink Dr. Pepper." [<Heb. נבא (prophesy)]

neb-bach (נעבאך) *n.* **1.** A pathetic, unsuccessful person: LOSER. "He's such a N., he could lose money by winning the lottery." *adv.* **2.** Unfortunately; as a cause for chagrin: REGRETTABLY. "Since his father is N. so poor, the yeshiva doesn't even mention tuition to him." [Etymology uncertain. Perhaps <HG Nebel (cloud) indicating a haziness or uncertainty, or <Russian НИ(not) + БОГ(divine) indicating a reluctance to ascribe such bad fortune to השי"ת] **Var.** lo yitzlach.

ne-gi-os (נגיעות) *n.* An association with another party possibly affecting decisions regarding that party: VESTED INTEREST, CONFLICT OF INTERESTS. "If you feel your chavrusashaft with him means that you have N., don't make any suggestions to him about how he should change his schedule for learning." [cf. noigeia]

neh-neh (נהנה) *p.a.(i)* To profit or gain: BENEFIT. "It's not right to take someone else's things even if you are not yourself N. from them." [cf. hanaa]

nem on (אנ-נעמען) *vt.* To assume to be true in the absence of verified proof or evidence: PRESUME. "Don't N. that Tosfos holds like you say until you've seen other places where he says so kluhr ois." [<Yid. <HG annehmen (accept)] **Var.** take on.

ne-mo-nus (נאמנות) *n.* Worthiness of belief: CREDIBILITY. "He lies all the time. How can you give him any N. on a question like this?" [<Heb. אמן (believe)]

ner-veiz (נערוועז) *Var. of* nervous.

ner-vous *adj.* **1.** Excessively excited: OVERWROUGHT. "Don't be N. about the darkness; it's just an eclipse." **2.** Disturbed due to displeasure or irritation: ANNOYED. "Don't be N. about the stale bread; it's just part of yeshiva life." *vt. phr.* **3. get, or make, nervous** To be disagreeable to one's liking: IRK. "Rebbe's constant repetitions get me N." [<Eng. emulative of Yid. נערוועז]

ne-ti-ya (נטייה) *n.* A preference based on personal disposition or leanings: PREDILECTION. "He has a N. toward less lomdishe sugyas." [cf. noite] —**N.B.** Often pl.: netiyos.

ne-vu-a (נבואה) *n.* Extrasensory knowledge of the future: PRECOGNI-TION. "I prepared an extra portion for dinner. I must have had a N. that you were coming." [cf. navi]

ni-kar (ניכר) *adj. (p.a. only)* **1.** Worthy of attracting attention: NOTICE-ABLE. "The damage wasn't even N., so I didn't report it to the insurance company." **2.** Readily or easily manifest or obvious: EVIDENT. "His midos are N. in the way he deals with others." **3.** Having a significant effect: CONSEQUENTIAL. "His mistake in the numbers was N., and the Menahel had some time explaining the discrepancy." [<Heb. נכר (recognize)]

ni-so-yen (נסיון) *n., pl.* **nisyoinos** A temptation or obstacle that, by moral imperative, must be overcome: CHAL-LENGE. "It's a N. to go to learn today when the weather is so nice." [<Heb.נסה (try)]

nis-poy-el (נתפעל) *Var. of* mispoyel.

noi-gei-a (נוגע) *p.a.(i)* **1.** To have relevancy: PERTAIN. "That Tosfos is not N. to this din." **2.** Able to be done: PRACTICAL. "I wanted to learn with him despite his tough schedule, but it's just not N." *p.a.(t)* **3.** To bear upon or to bring about a change in: AFFECT. "I only looked in the records for information that's N. me." *adj. (p.a. only)* **4.** Usually "a nogeia" Related in a way as would affect an opinion: AS-SOCIATED. "They didn't let him on the planning committee because he was a N." [<Heb.נגע (touch)] **Var. for def. 4** noigeia bedavar.

noi-gei-a be-da-var (נוגע בדבר) *Var. of* noigeia, def. 4.

noi-heg (נוהג) *adv., conjugated as a p.a. followed by an infinitive* **1.** As a matter of common practice: HABITU-ALLY. "I'm N. to sleep with the windows open, even in the winter." **2.** As a matter of religious custom, as distinguished from law; or, in a manner protective of religious law though not integral to it: TRADITIONALLY, FAITHFULLY. "I'm N. to eat fish every Shabbos." *p.a.(i)* **3.** To conduct oneself in accordance with a pattern: BEHAVE. "If you're N. in a good way, mimeila people will think well of you." [<Heb. נהג (lead)]

noi-te (נוטה) *p.a.(i)* **1.** To have a predilection or tendency to engage in or to partake of: LEAN. "Although his father is a poisek, he was always more N. toward lomdus than to halacha." *Followed by "to" or "toward," which is elided in translation* **2.** To find more agreeable than: PREFER. "As a mashgiach for kashrus he's surrounded by fine food, but he's N. to hot dogs and fries." [<Heb. נטה (stray)]

nor-mahl(e) (נארמאהל) *adj.* **1.** Habitual or customary: USUAL, NOT UNUSUAL. "In our yeshiva, it's N. to get kicked out for almost anything." **2.** Displaying reason or good sense: RATIONAL. "He's been in learning for years; it's not N. to expect anyone just to give him a good job with no experience." **3.** Conforming to standard, expected, or typical conventions or patterns: ORDINARY. "Instead of trying all these fancy recipes, the restaurant should just make a N. meal at a good price." [<Eng. normal emulative of <Yid.] **Var.** normal.

nor-mal *Var. of* normahl(e)

nunt(e) (נאהענט) *adj.* Marked by intimacy of acquaintance, association, or familiarity: CLOSE. "That bochur is very N. with the one uncle who always sends him money."

nu-sach (נוסח) *n., pl.* **nuschaos** Uniform or standard expression: FORMAT, FORMULA. "Don't even ask the Mashgiach for reshus to go; he'll just turn you down with his usual N. about how your place is in the yeshiva." [<Heb. שׂוח (discuss)] **Var.** girsa.

O

of-en ort (אויפֿן ארט) *adv.* **1.** In reference to a written citation, to or at the place: AD LOCUM. "Look up the mekor, and you'll see that he answers O." **2.** Without hesitation: IMMEDIATELY. "He knows those halachos kluhr, and he answered my shaila O." [<Yid. <HG auf den ort (at the place)]

oib a-zoi (אויב אזוי) *conj.* By logical inference: CONSEQUENTLY. "The Rosh Yeshiva said we can go? O. we might as well leave right away." [<Yid. <HG ob (if) + cf. azoi]

oi-fen (אופֿן) *n., pl.* **oifanim 1.** A quality of individuality: STYLE. "He dresses in a certain O. You can't miss him in a crowd." **2.** A distinctive way of doing something or of causing something to happen: MANNER. "He teaches in such a complicated O. that he loses everyone in minutes." **3.** A set of circumstances or state of affairs: INSTANCE. "If it's an O. of self-defense, you can do almost anything to protect yourself." [<Heb. אופֿן (wheel)]

oi-lam (עולם) *n.* **1.** A particular class with common interests, aims, goals, etc.: WORLD. "The yeshivishe O. doesn't watch TV." **2.** A group of people who associate because of common purposes, philosophies, interests, etc.: COTERIE. "The halacha O. usually ignores the Aggadetas." **3.** A group of people, mostly young, who associate on a social (rather than criminal) basis: GANG. "The O. gets together to walk on Shabbos." **4.** Persons who partake of or share in a certain matter: PARTICIPANTS. "The O. in that shul talks too much." [<Heb. עולם (universe)]
—N.B. Note that for def. 4, "oilam" is singular while its translation is plural.

oi-med (עומד) *p.a.(i)* To discuss or consider intently: DELIBERATE. "I haven't really been O. on that inyan, but I can give you some of the basics." [<Heb. עמד (stand)]

oi-nes (אונס) *n.* **1.** A situation compelling the performance of an undesirable act: MATTER OF NECESSITY. "I had to catch a flight, so davening without a minyan was an O." **2.** One who, under duress, performs an undesirable act: VICTIM OF CIRCUMSTANCES. "I was an O. and had to daven in the airport without a minyan." [<Heb. אנס (force)] **Var. for def. 2** onus.

ois (אויס) *prefix* Previously; erstwhile; no longer: EX-. "He can't help you get into that yeshiva. He's already O. macher." [<Yid. <HG aus (out)] **—N.B.** Note the need for the English indefinite article in translation.

oi-sek (עוסק) *p.a.(i)* Concerned, committed, or engaged: INVOLVED. "I don't have time for nonsense; I'm O. in learning." [cf. eisek]

ois-ge-ar-bit(e) (אויס-געארבעט) *adj.* **1.** Having or showing control of one's feelings, behavior, or attitude: SELF-POSSESSED. "He's so O. largely because of all the musar he's learned." **2.** Highly regarded, thought about, and decided upon with deliberation: CONSIDERED. "The O. likut deals with the whole inyan in a very mesudardike oifen." [<Yid. <HG arbeiten (work)]

ois-ge-halt-en(e) (אויסגעהאלטען) *adj.* **1.** Worthy of trust and confidence: TRUSTWORTHY. "In this kehilla, the butcher is O." **2.** Soundly concluded, able to withstand question or doubt: FIRM, CONFIRMED. "His shita in kashrus is O. by all the modern teshuvos." [<Yid. <HG halten (hold)]

ois-ge-re-chened (אויסגערעכענט) *adj.* Premeditated, considered in advance: CALCULATED. "His way of paskening is very O. and rarely creates controversy." [<Yid. <HG rechnen (count)]

ois-ge-vept(e) (אויסגעוועפט) *adj.* **1.** Having lost one's animation due to fatigue: BEAT. "He was O. after the long game." **2.** Marked by a decline in physical and mental faculties due to old age: FEEBLE. "The O. substitute let the class out early." **3.** Having lost strength or freshness: LIMP. "You've left the cap off too long; the soda's O." [cf. vep]

ois varf (אויס-ווארף) *n.* One who is undesirable because of such character, views, or behavior as are considered unacceptable: REJECT. "Ever since they heard he'd been at the beach, he was branded an O." [<Yid. <HG auswerfen (throw out)]

o-nus (אנוס) *Var. of* oines, def. 2.

oo-lai (אולי) *adv.* **1.** Not for certain: POSSIBLY. "O. I'll go home for Shabbos. The Mashgiach didn't exactly say 'no.'" **2.** Possible, but not likely to occur or to be true: IMPROBABLY. "I don't think you're 100% right, but O. your taina has some merit." [<Heb. אולי (perhaps)]

out-of-town *n. & adv.* Anywhere but New York City: SOMEWHERE ELSE. "He learns eppis in London. Dacht zich that's O." [<Eng.]

P

par-sha (פרשה) *n.* **1.** A subject of conversation: TOPIC. "You're not even in this P., so don't offer your opinions." **2.** General realm of feasibility: BALLPARK. "Don't give up trying to win the contest; you're still in the P." **3.** A tedious, lengthy enumeration or account: LITANY. "Rebbe gave me a whole P. for coming late." [<Heb. פרש (separate)] **Var. for def. 3** shtikl Torah, mishebeirach.

pas (פאסען) *vi.* **1.** To be suitable or fitting: BEFIT, GO, or [as *p.a.(i)*] BE APPROPRIATE. "It didn't P. for a Rav to get into such a silly argument with that loud balebus." *p.a.(t)* **2.** To fit the definition of: BE TANTAMOUNT TO. "Despite the proof, the Beis Din thought it didn't P. geneiva." [<Yid. <HG passen (fit)]

pash-tus (פשטות) *n.* **1.** That which is taken for granted: ASSUMPTION. "The P. is that he doesn't know any more about this than about anything else he talks about." *adv.* **2.** Based upon assumption: OFFHAND. "P. I

would say that you can't all fit into that small car." [<Emulative of Heb. פשט (straight)] **Var. for def. 2** bifshitus.

pas-ken (פסק׳נען) *vt. & vi.* To reach an authoritative decision on a matter, often of halacha: DECIDE, CONCLUDE. "The Rav P. as his balebatim wanted; that's how he kept his job." [<Yid. <Heb. פסק (cut)]

pa-ter (פאטר׳ן) *vt.* **1.** To exonerate from an offense: EXCUSE. "I don't think that your explanation will be enough for the Mashgiach to P. you from a knas." **2.** To dismiss or release from an obligation: EXEMPT. "Since the trial would last over Shabbos, the judge P. him from jury duty." *Usually followed by "up"* **3.** To render available: FREE. "I'll join you later if I can P. up some time." [<Yid. <cf. potur]

pe-le (פלא) *n.* **1.** That which elicits surprise or admiration: WONDER. "The new skyscraper is a P. of engineering." **2.** That which is enigmatic or difficult to understand: MYS-

77

TERY. "How he got here so fast from so far away is a P." [<Heb. פלא (marvel)]

pe-le-dik(e) *adj.* **1.** Eliciting wonder or admiration: MARVELOUS. "He has a P. way of being mazbir shveire gemaros so that anyone can understand them." **2.** Difficult to understand the rationale for: INCOMPREHENSIBLE. "It's P. to think that people could be dumb enough to believe what missionaries tell them." [cf. pele]

pe-u-la (פעולה) *n.* **1.** The performance of a specified thing: ACTION. "You can't expect the project to get started without some P." **2.** Involvement in the accomplishment of goals: ACTIVITY. "The man's P. for the yeshiva increased the fundraising efforts." [<Heb. פעל (act)]

pis-choin peh (פתחון פה) *n.* Basis to comment: GROUNDS, LEVERAGE. "My chavrusa's pshat left me with no P." [<Heb. פתח (open) + פה (mouth)]

po-shut (פשוט) *adv.* Being without complication or complexity: SIMPLY. "He answered P. and didn't need to come on to major lomdus." [cf. poshut(e)]

po-shut(e) (פשוט) *adj.* **1.** Neither complicated nor complex: SIMPLE. "I can't believe Rebbe gave such a P. test; everyone passed." **2.** Without special pretensions or superiority: PLAIN. "He's a P. person who works hard and lives within his means." [<Heb. פשט (straight)]

po-tur (פטור) *adj.* *(p.a. only)* Excused from or not responsible for: FREE, OFF THE HOOK. "As long as I take the tests, the Menahel said I'm P. from English." [<Heb. פטר (free)]

poy-el ois (אויספועל'ן) *vi.* **1.** To accomplish a specific goal: SUCCEED. "After applying for five years, he finally P. at getting an apartment close to yeshiva." *vt.* **2.** To succeed in attaining through effort: ACHIEVE, PULL OFF. "He worked hard and P. a big raise." [cf. peula + cf. ois] **Cf.** tu oif, def. 1.

praht (פרט) *n., pl.* **pruttim,** An element considered distinctly and in relation to a whole: DETAIL. "Rebbe said I should just go vaiter and not get stuck on every P." [<Aram. פרט (divide)]

prahv (פראווען) *vt.* To carry out: PERFORM. "I'm too shy to P. any shtik at a chassuna." [<Yid. <Slavic (?)]

pri-va-tish(e) (פריוואטיש) *adj.* Of the property or privity owned by, intended for, or restricted to a particular individual: PERSONAL. "Don't read my mail; it's P." [<Eng. "private" emulating Yiddish]

prust(e) (פראסט) *adj.* Lewd or base: VULGAR. "Only a P. guy could tell a joke like that in yeshiva." [<Yid. <Heb. פרץ (unfettered)]

pshat (פשט) *n.* **1.** A manner fitting an explanation into the words of a difficult text: RENDERING. "His convoluted P. in the sugya makes you wonder if he's learning the same daf as everyone else." **2.** An explanation of the logic behind or the source of a passage, event, work, etc.: METHOD, INTERPRETATION. "I once had a shiduch in an art museum, and I made up P. in all the paintings to try to make an impression." **3.** That which explains the rationale for something: JUSTIFICATION, REASON. "I thought they're friends; what's the P. they're fighting?" [<Heb. פשט (straight)] **Cf.** what's pshat.

—**N.B.** Defs. 2 and 3 may require the English definite article in translation.

p-tur (פטור) *n.* **1.** A release from liability or obligation: EXEMPTION. "I need a doctor's note as a P. from going to class." **2.** That which renders one free from an offense: EXCUSE. "My P. for coming late was that I couldn't get a ride back from out of town." [cf. potur]

punkt (פונקט) *adv.* Precisely, as in time or place: EXACTLY. "Our teacher shows up P. at 3:17 every day." [<Yid. <HG Punkt (point)]

R

ra-ash (רעש) *n.* Intensive discussion and debate pursuant to some surprising or disturbing turn of events: COMMOTION. "The R. over the earlier curfew made the Mashgiach have second thoughts." [<Heb. רעש (noise)]

rach-mo-nus (רחמנות) *n* **in the phrase, "to have rachmonus on" 1.** Mercy: COMPASSION. "The older bochrim finally had R. on the new student and stopped teasing him." **2.** A situation deserving of compassion: PITY. "It's a R. to see all the hungry, stray cats hanging around by the yeshiva's garbage." **3.** A person worthy of compassion: NE'ER-DO-WELL. "He's already over thirty and can't make a proper living. He's a real R." [<Heb. רחם (love)] **Cf.** nebbach.

ra-ya (ראיה) *n.* **1.** Ground for belief; that which proves or disproves: EVIDENCE, SUPPORT. "One obscure Medrash is his only R. for his big chidush." **2.** That which serves to point out: INDICATION. "That the bochur has no fever is no R. that he isn't really sick." [<Heb. ראה (see)]

re-chen (רעכנען) *vt.* **1.** To determine or estimate by reason, common sense, or experience: RECKON. "The yeshiva R. that only twelve new bochrim would be coming, but over thirty actually came." **2.** To compute mathematically: CALCULATE. "The bookkeeper R. all the checks that came in as a result of the appeal." [<Yid. <HG rechnen (figure)]

re-ga (רגע) *n.* **1.** A short span of time: MOMENT. "I was only gone for a R. before someone took my shtender." *usually preceded by "a," interj.* **2.** A request for patience or time: HOLD ON. "R. Let's figure out where we're going to meet before we split up." [<Heb. רגע (moment)]

reid (רעהד) *n.* Unofficial information spread through the grapevine: HEARSAY. "The R. around the Beis Medrash is that Rebbe is starting his own yeshiva." [<Yid. <HG reden (talk)]

81

reitz on (אנרייצען) *vt.* To irritate or provoke with persistent annoyance or teasing: ANTAGONIZE. "The neighborhood kids sometimes R. the bochrim and then run away." [<Yid. <HG reizen (irritate)]

re-mez (רמז) *n., pl.* **remuzim 1.** A mark or detail from which the existence of an implicit piece of information can be drawn: TRACE. "He never used that gematria as a raya for his chidush; he said it was just a R." **2.** A mark or detail that suggests the existence of implicit information: ALLUSION. "The Medrash was a R. to the need for teshuva." [<Heb. רמז (hint)]

re-shus (רשות) *n., pl.* **reshuyos 1.** Consent, especially formal: LICENSE, PERMISSION. "No matter how I begged, the Mashgiach wouldn't give me R. to go to the chassuna." **2.** The right and power to command, enforce, or grant: AUTHORIZATION. "Don't worry; only the Rosh Yeshiva, not the principal, has the R. to suspend you from school." **3.** Territory or range of control: DOMAIN. "I told my roommate to keep his dirty laundry out of my R." [<Heb. רשה (power)]

rie-zig(e) (ריעזיג) *adj.* **1.** Remarkable for great size or number: SIZABLE. "A R. crowd shows up daily for the Daf Yomi." **2.** Remarkable for excellence: SUPERIOR. "Our shiur is very lucky to have such a R. Rebbe." [<Yid. <HG Riese (giant)]
—**N.B.** As an interjection: GREAT!

rish-us (רשעות) *n.* **1.** An unreasonable desire to see another suffer: MALICE. "Hitler's R. is recognized by even the least sympathetic goyim." **2.** Pain or distress willfully caused to others: CRUELTY. "Simple R. made the teacher give us extra homework." [<Heb. רשע (wicked)]

roiv (רוב) *n.* **1.** The larger portion or number: MAJORITY. "Traditionally Beis Din paskens by the R." *adj.* **2.** The majority of: MOST. "R. bochrim come from New York, but some of the out-of-towners can really learn well." [<Heb. רב (great)]

ru-ach (רוח) *n.* Characteristic underlying feeling or tone: ETHOS, ESPRIT DE CORPS. "The R. in our shiur really enhances our learning." [<Heb. רוח (wind)]

ru-gil (רגיל) *adj. (p.a. only)* **1.** As a matter of habit: WONT. "I'm R. to wake up for shachris with or without an alarm clock." **2.** Occurring habitually or with frequency: COMMON. "It's R. for bochrim to complain about yeshiva food no matter how hard the cook tries." [<Heb. רגל (foot)]

S

sai ve sai (סיי ווו סיי) *adv.* At any rate; in any event: ANYHOW, WHATEVER. "Say whatever you want about him; I like him S." [<Yid. <HG sowieso (thus as thus)] **Var.** sai vi.

sai vi *Var. of* sai ve sai.

sa-ka-na (סכנה) *n.* Exposure to peril or danger: RISK, HAZARD. "It's a S. to go into that neighborhood at night." [<Heb. סכן (perplexity, danger)] **—N.B.** "makom sakana" refers to a situation in which danger is prevalent, i.e., "dangerous place."

say (or say inside) *vt.* **1.** To read a text, especially pertaining to Torah subjects, aloud and to provide a simultaneous explanation: RECITE. "Rebbe davka asked me to S. the gemara inside because he knew I was prepared." **say over (or say outside) 2.** To provide a concise restatement of the main or salient points: RECAPITULATE, SUMMARIZE. "I asked Rebbe just to S. over the sugya, so I could get right to the Tosfos." **say over or (tell over) 3.** To relate an incident: RECOUNT.

"He couldn't wait to get back so he could S. over the maise to his chavrusa." [<Eng.]

se-der (סדר) *n., pl.* **sdorim 1.** Established way, method, or rule: ORDER (LINESS), SYSTEM. "My roommate has such a S. that I'm afraid to move anything." **2.** A series of things to be done within a given period of time: ROUTINE. "The S. in yeshiva is: shachris, halacha, breakfast, chazora, shiur, lunch, mincha, musar, bekius, English, dinner, chumash, shmooze, lomdus, maariv." **3.** A scheduled time for learning Torah: PERIOD. "I usually do the Daf Yomi during our bekius S." [<Heb. סדר (arrange)] **Var. for def. 2** seder hayom. **—N.B.** "bein hasdorim" is the scheduled break between sdorim, i.e., "recess."

se-fer (ספר) *n., pl.* **sforim** A literary composition written particularly of, on, or about the Torah: BOOK. "If you bring me the S., I can show you where he says it befeirush."

—**N.B.** The phrase "in sefer" refers to a comment of the author himself rather than to a comment recorded from hearsay or extracted from other works. "That pshat is Reb Chaim in sefer."

sei-chel (שכל) *n.* **1.** Intelligence or acumen: BRAINS. "It doesn't take much S. not to walk barefoot in the snow." **2.** The mental capacity to discern and work through processes: REASON. "Use a little S. and try not to get excited when you reach a hard part in the Tosfos." [<Heb. שכל (intellect)]

sfehlt (ס'פעהלט) **Cf.** fehlt.

shaf (שאפען) *vt.* **1.** To obtain or achieve by particular care and effort (often by cunning): PROCURE. "The bochrim S. some extra cole slaw when the cook wasn't watching." **2.** To produce through cognitive skills: EFFECT. "He didn't really answer the stira; he just S. a chiluk between the sugyas." *n.* **3.** Desideratum obtained by some cunning method of procurement: ACQUISITION. "This watch was a great S.; I paid $100, but it's zicher worth $500." [<Yid. <HG schaffen (to put, do)]

shai-chus (שייכות) *n.* **1.** Connection or relationship: ASSOCIATION, CORRELATION. "He compares the two sugyas, but I can't see the S. between them." **2.** Understanding, grasp, or ability: INKLING. "I'm into Chasidus, but I have no S. to the kabala you need to know." **3.** Pertinence or connectedness to the matter at hand: RELEVANCE. "I hear what you're saying, but what's the S. to what I said?" **4.** Friendship or intimacy: CLOSENESS, COMMUNICATION. "He keeps a S. with his old chavrusa even though they haven't learned together for years." *In the phrase "to have shaichus"* **5. a.** Some effect upon: BEARING. Your suggestion has no S. to my situation." **b.** To be associated through dealings with: TO HAVE TO DO WITH. "I've always liked him, but I don't have much S. with him." [cf. shayach] **Var. for defs. 1, 3, 4, and 6** kesher.

shai-la (שאילה) *n.* **1.** A question posed to resolve a doubt, often specifically regarding a matter of learning or halacha: QUERY. "My Rav will never answer a S. on business without consultation." **ask a shaila 2.** To discuss in order to receive advice or wisdom from an authority: CONSULT. "I couldn't change my career without asking a S." [<Heb. שאל (ask)]

sharf(e) (שאַרף) *adj.* Acute or clever: PENETRATING. "He was embarrassed by the S. insult because he knew it was right." [<Yid. <HG scharf (sharp)]

sharf-e (שאַרפּע) *n.* A person noted for deep penetrating observation: SMART ALECK. "No one wants to start up with him because he's such a S." [cf. sharf(e)]

shatz up (אפשאצעז) *vt.* To determine or estimate the worth of: EVALUATE. "We S. how long it would take us to finish the Daf, but it took much longer." [<Yid. <HG schatzen (gauge)]

sha-yach (שייך) *adj. (p.a. only)* **1.** Capable of being true or believable: CONCEIVABLE. "It's not S. that someone can jump over that hurdle." **2.** Capable of being done: SURMOUNTABLE. "This puzzle is so hard, it's not S." **3.** Practical, reasonable, or possible: FEASIBLE. "I tried to find time to learn with him, but it wasn't S." [<Aram. שוך (connect)]

she-boi (שבו) *adj. (noun complement only)* Noteworthy of or distinctive to something: OF IT, IN IT. "Everyone is raving about the new tape, but I don't see the gadlus S." [<Heb. שבו (which is in it)]

she-i-fos (שאיפות) *n.* A strong desire to achieve greatness: ASPIRATIONS. "My chavrusa has S. to be a Rosh Yeshiva." [<Heb. שאף (respire)]

shem (שם) *n., pl.* **sheimos 1.** An assessment of one's character: REPUTATION. "The yeshiva has a good S., and bochrim from everywhere try to get in." **2.** A name describing the nature of a subject: TITLE OF. "By paying so much attention to the grammar in Rashi, he got a S. baal dikduk." **shem davar 3. a.** That which is significant or important: PROMINENT FEATURE. "Wheat is a S. davar in Kansas." **b.** That

for which something is famous or well-known: SPECIALTY. "Wine is a S. davar in France." [<Heb. שם (name)]

shi-duch (שידוך) *n., pl.* **shiduchim 1.** A fitting marital match: MATE. "She was a perfect S. for him; they seem so happy." **2.** A preappointed meeting for the purpose of possible marriage: DATE. "I can't take you with me; I'm going for a S." **3.** An association as that of partners: PARTNERSHIP. "The two businessmen are a great S., and they are very successful as a result." [<Aram. שדך (negotiate)]

shie-bud (שיעבוד) *n., pl.* **shibudim 1.** The legal claim upon the property of another for the payment of a debt: LIEN. "I have a S. on my car for all my outstanding tickets." **2.** A moral or legal duty: OBLIGATION. "He has a S. to his goyishe neighbor to shovel snow on Sundays since the neighbor does it on Shabbos." [<Aram. <Heb. עבד (work)]

shi-ta (שיטה) *n.* **1.** An opinion or judgment colored by the predilection of its proponent: POSITION. "Reb Yochanan's S. is that he can keep the cheftza without finding the owner." **2.** A guiding rule: PRINCIPLE. "I have a S. not to smoke in the dorm even after the Mashgiach leaves." [<Aram. שוט (row, line)]

shi-tos (שיטות) *n. (conjugated as plural)* A system of doctrines, criteria, convictions, or principles that colors

its proponent's perspectives: EPIS-TEMOLOGY, DOGMAS. "Maybe he can't find a shiduch because he has so many S." [cf. shita]
—N.B. "baal shita" refers to the proponent of such a system and implies that the proponent is particularly picky or overly selective.

shi-ur (שיעור) *n., pl.* **shiurim 1.** A quantity or measure: AMOUNT. "If you don't have a proper S., you might have to do the mitzva again." **2.** A discourse on any Torah subject: LECTURE. "He tried to say a S. on Chumash, but his lomdus S. is much better." **3.** A step or degree in rank, particularly as a measure of advancement through school or yeshiva: GRADE. "He is younger than the rest of his S., but he gets along with the other bochrim." [<Heb. שער (gate)]

shkoy-ach (יישר כחך) *Interj.* A polite expression of approval or gratitude: THANKS, WELL DONE, CONGRATULATIONS. "S. for fixing my bike; I'll pay you later." [cf. yashrus + cf. koyach, see מס שבת פז.]

shlep (שלעפען) *vt.* **1.** To move with great effort: DRAG. "I had to S. the same box up and down the stairs." *vi.* **2.** To move oneself with great or undue effort: TRUDGE. "I S. to the airport for nothing. The flight was canceled." *n.* **3.** That which requires excessive effort: INCONVENIENCE. "It was a big S. to arrange all the rooms for the guests." [<Yid. <HG schleppen (drag)]

shli-ta (שליטה) *n.* **1.** The power to rule, whether assumed or not: AUTHORITY. "That teacher really enjoys the S. he has over the bochrim during class." **2.** A restraining and dominating influence over a person, object, or situation: CONTROL. "My father has incredible S. over his car, even at night or in the rain." [<Heb. שלט (rule)]

shluf (שלאפען) *n.* **1.** A short, refreshing period of sleep: NAP. "I'm glad I could chap a S. on the train." **2.** Deep, refreshing sleep: SLUMBER. "I had too good a S. last night to be tired today." [<Yid. <HG schlafen (sleep)]

shlug up (אפשלאגען) *vt.* To prove an assertion false and thus to render ineffective a claim based upon it: NEGATE, DISCREDIT. "Once my chavrusa showed me the sefer, I had to admit that he S. my pshat." [<Yid. <HG schlagen (hit)]

shmaltz-ing (שמאלץ) *adj. (p.a. only)* **1.** Perspiring profusely: DRENCHED. "We were S. when the air conditioner died." **2.** Oppressively hot: SWELTERING. "The summer weather was too S. to be comfortable for outside activities." [<Yid. <HG schmaltz (grease)]

shmek (שמעקען) *vt.* **1.** To discern by the olfactory sense: SMELL. "You can S. the yeshiva's chulnt all over the neighborhood." *vi.* **2.** To exude an odor: SMELL. "The neighborhood S. from the yeshiva's chulnt." **3.** To hint or suggest: SMACK. "Your attitude S. of gaiva." *vt. & vi.* **shmek ois 4.** To notice the evidence of: SUSPECT, FIGURE OUT. "Although I haven't told him, I think my chavrusa S. that I'm looking to learn with someone else." [<Yid. <HG schmecken (smell)]

shmooze (שמועס) *n., pl.* **shmoozen 1.** Any serious talk or discussion on a moral or ethical issue: SERMON. "The Mashgiach gave an incredible S. on the need for teshuva." **2.** An informal conversation: CHAT. "I can't say I know from just the quick S. I had with him." *vi.* **3.** To converse informally; to chat or prattle: CHATTER. "If he didn't always S. with the guy next to him, he might chap shiur better." **shmooze out 4.** To scold mildly: CHIDE. "I would S. him out if I thought it would make him come to his senses." [<Yid. <Heb. שמועות, cf. shmua]

shmu-a (שמועה) *n.* Unverified information learned from questionable sources: RUMOR. "There's a S. around that, during shiur, the Mashgiach looks through the dorm for food and radios." [<Heb. שמע (hear)]

shmutz (שמוץ) *n.* **1.** Foul or filthy substance: DIRT. "If you bring any S. into my house, you'll have to clean it up." **2.** Vulgar or obscene language or thought: SMUT, FILTH. "If you bring any S. into my house, you'll be thrown right out." [<Yid. <HG Schmutz (dirt)]

shmutz-ik(e) (שמוציג) *adj.* **1.** Severely soiled or dirty: FILTHY. "When clothes are that S., it hardly pays to wash them." **2.** Indecent, vulgar, or obscene: SMUTTY. "This book is too S. for even a public-school class to read." [cf. shmutz]

shnar (שנארען) *vt. & vi.* To request to obtain without payment: MOOCH. "Every time I buy some chocolate, someone comes to S." [<Yid. <HG schnorren (cadge)]

shnarer (שנארער) One who requests to receive without payment: LEECH. "Just get your own snacks. I can't deal with a S. like you." [cf. shnar]

shnit (שניט) *n.* Distinguishing style: MODE. "Some out-of-towners have a distaste for the bochrim with that New York S." [<Yid. <HG Schnitt (incision)]

shoin (שוין) *interj.* **1.** Stop for now: ENOUGH. "S. Stop arguing and go vaiter." *adv.* **2.** Just previously to an appointed time: ALREADY. "We just started learning, and seder is S. over." [<Yid. <HG schon (already)]

shoi-resh (שרש) *n., pl.* **sharushim 1.** The uninflected form of a word: STEM, INFINITIVE. "To figure out a word's meaning, first find the S." **2.** The central or essential point: KERNEL. "The S. of the electrical problem was a mystery to even the chief electrician." **3.** The point from which something comes or is obtained: SOURCE. "We traced the gemara to its S. in Chumash." [<Heb. שרש (root)]

shoi-te (שוטה) *n., pl.* **shoitim** One who acts foolishly or unreasonably: FOOL. "Only a S. would touch that wire with his bare hands." [<Heb. שטה (insane)]

shpar (שפארען) *vt.* To reach by deduction: EXTRAPOLATE. "He S. the whole chidush from a maise rather than from mekoros." [<Yid. <HG spören (spur)]

shpitz (שפיץ) *adj. (p.a. only) or* **shpitzy** *before a noun* **1.** Elegant or classy: COOL. "His tie is S. and must have cost a lot." *adv.* **2.** Perfectly or in harmony with an ideal: DEFINITIVELY. "His ties are always S. cool." [<Yid. <HG spitz (acute)]

shprach (שפראך) *n., pl.* **shprachen 1.** A collection of words that carry with them a meaning and connotations specific to a particular group: ARGOT. "His paper got an 'F' because it was peppered with the yeshivishe S." **2.** A quote or emulation of a particular linguistic style: DICTION. "He wrote with an achroinishe S. to make his sefer sound more lomdish." [<Yid. <HG Sprache (speech)]

shrai (שרייען) *n.* **1.** A loud cry in anger, pain, fear, surprise, etc.: SCREAM. "I heard a S. at night that scared me out of my mind." *vi.* **2.** To call or scream: SHOUT. "That kid S. at night just

to wake everyone up." [<Yid. <HG schreien (call out)]

shrek (שרעק) *interj.* Expression of consternation: OH NO! "S., I left my wallet back in the dorm." [<Yid. <HG Schreck (fright)]

shrek-lich(e) (שרעקליך) *adj.* Awful or frightening: TERRIBLE. "I had a S. headache and couldn't go to seder." [cf. shrek]

shtaig (שטייגען) *vi.* To work one's way up: ADVANCE, PROGRESS. "You can S. with every moment of learning." [<Yid. <HG steigen (climb)]

shtam (שטאמען) *vi.* To take origin or to rise from: STEM. "His fatigue S. from the long hours he spends in Beis Medrash." [<Yid. <HG stammen (derive)]

shtark (שטארק) *adv.* With intensity and regularity: STEADFASTLY. "As long as my son is learning S., I want him to stay in yeshiva." [<Yid. <HG stark (strong)]

shtark(e) (שטארק) *adj.* **1.** Solid in construction: STURDY. "The earthquake didn't effect the Beis Medrash's S. walls." **2.** Of great force: POWERFUL. "The S. punch knocked him cold." **3.** Having great bodily or muscular power: STRONG. "The younger bochrim feel safer walking with the S. older guys." **4.** Emotionally moving: INSPIRING. "The Mashgiach gave a

S. shmooze last night." **5.** Striving to learn Torah: SERIOUS. "Some of the S. bochrim learn all night." **6.** Unusually good of its kind: TOP-NOTCH. "That's a S. derech for learning Daf Yomi without forgetting too much." **7.** Marked by significant achievement or attainment of goals: SUCCESSFUL. "I'm happy my son is having such a S. zman." [cf. shtark]

shtark-en (שטאַרקענען) *vt.* **1.** To strengthen the learning of: STIMULATE. "Toward the end of the zman, you have to S. the bochrim a little." **2.** To bring consolation or hope to: COMFORT. "It's proper to S. someone who has an unfortunate tragedy." **3.** To strengthen the physical properties of: BRACE. "We need to S. the sukkah if we don't want it to fall." [cf. shtark]

shtat-i (שטאַטליך) *adj.* Fine or imposing in appearance, quality, or impression: STATELY, URBANE. "The guy looks a little too S. in his Cadillac for a guy who's supposed to be in kollel." [<Yid. <HG Staat (state)] **Var.** shtats.

shtats *Var. of* shtati.

shtel (שטעלען) **Cf.** shtel zich.

shtel avek (אוועקשטעלען) *vt.* **1.** To put away for future use: STORE. "We just S. these dishes until next Pesach." **2.** To bring up through association of ideas: SUGGEST. "You can't just S. a yesoid without checking other

mekoros." [<Yid. <HG stellen (to place)]

shtel-er (שטעלער) *n.* A job, particularly one within Orthodox religious education: POSITION. "My brother got a S. teaching in the new yeshiva." [cf. shtel avek.]

shtel tzu (צושטעלען) *vt.* To represent as similar: LIKEN. "Everyone tries to S. his situation to Jewish history, but the Yidden are unique." [cf. shtel avek]

shtel zich (זיך-שטעלען) *reflexive verb* To assign oneself to a specific purpose: APPLY ONESELF. "If he S. to the sugya, he'll be able to learn it on his own." [cf. shtel avek] —**N.B.** May elide "zich."

shtend-er (שטענדער) *n.* A desk or lectern with a slanted top, intended for reading while standing or sitting: STAND. "Every time I leave my place to get a sefer, someone chaps my S." [<Yid. <HG stehen (to stand)]

shter (שטערען) *vt.* **1.** To disturb or annoy: BOTHER. "Stop S. us by drumming on the desk." **2.** To interfere with or break into, as in a conversation: INTERRUPT. "Don't S. the shiur with all your simple kashes." *n.* **3.** An annoyance or disturbance: NUISANCE. "His drumming was a S. to my concentration." **4.** An object or person interrupting: INTERFERENCE. "My kid brother is always a S. to my learning." [<Yid. <HG stören (disturb)]

shtik (שטיק) *adj.* **1.** A portion or quantity of: PIECE OF. "There's nothing like a S. potato kugel on a cold day." **2.** (in the phrase "a shtik") Complete or total: EXEMPLARY (OF). "He may not be good at lomdus, but he's a S. bukki." *n.* **3.** Humorous or clever actions or ideas: PRANKS, ROUTINE. "The shnarer comes to yeshiva every year with the same made-up sympathy S." [<Yid. <HG Stück (piece)] **Var.** meshugas. —**N.B.** "shtikl" is a diminutive form for def. 1.

shtik-ky (שטיק) *adj.* Humorous or clever, referring to a person, idea, or concept: WITTY. "I have to admit it; your glow-in-the-dark Mickey Mouse tie is really S." [cf. shtik]

shtik-l (שטיק) *adj.* **1.** (in the phrase "a shtikl") To some degree or measure: SOMEWHAT, A BIT OF A(N). "He was a S. mad when he found the scratch on his car." [cf. shtik]

shtik-l Torah *Var. of* torah.

shtoch (שטאך) *vt.* **1.** To mock in a clever, ironic, and intentionally painful manner: INSULT. "If you want to S. him, mention his hairline." *n.* **2.** A clever, mocking, and usually ironic remark: JAB, BARB. "No matter how subtly he said it, I know it was intended as a S. " [<Yid. <HG stechen (stitch)] **Var. for def. 1** shtoch out.

shtoch out *Var. of* shtoch, def. 1.

shtoltz (שטאלץ) *n.* Character reflecting self-assuredness and commanding respect: DIGNITY. "If you maintain a little S., people will take you more seriously." [<Yid. <HG Stolz (pride)]

shtoltz-y (שטאלצִיג) *adj.* Possessing the characteristics of dignity and security: SELF-ASSURED. "He was S. enough for people to take note of him." [cf. shtoltz]

shtus (שטות) *n., pl.* **shtusim** The state or quality of lacking common sense or good judgment; the state or quality of being foolish: FOLLY, NONSENSE. "It's a S. not to pack warm clothes if you're going to the mountains." [cf. shoite]

shud (שאדען) *n.* Unlucky event or situation: SHAME, MISFORTUNE. "It's a S. to miss school for just a little snow." [<Yid. <HG schaden (harm)]

shvach (שבח) *n.* Praise of inherent worth: COMPLIMENT. "Believe it or not, I meant it as a S., not a shtoch, when I said that your shirt isn't ironed. I meant that you have no time for such gashmius." [<Heb. שבח (praise)]

shvach(e) (שוואך) *adj.* **1.** Slow to understand: DULL. "How can such a shtarke bochur learn with such a S. one?" **2.** Unacceptably lacking in seriousness: FRIVOLOUS. "He's a S. bochur and spends more time shopping than in the Beis Medrash." **3.** Lacking validity or strength: FLIMSY. "This chair is too S. to stand on." **4.** Having no lasting impression or influence: PROSAIC. "A S. Shabbos HaGadol drasha is a big letdown." **5.** Feeble or weak of body or health: INFIRM. "I was too S. to go back to yeshiva after my surgery." **6.** Lacking quality: POOR. "There's nothing to chazer after such a S. shiur." **7.** Marked by the failure to accomplish desired goals: UNSUCCESSFUL. "He had a S. zman because of all the distractions." **8.** Thinly scattered: SPARSE. "There was a S. turnout at the dinner, and the yeshiva was lucky not to lose money on the event." [<Yid. <HG schwache (weak)]

shver(e) (שוועהר) *adj.* **1.** Complicated, intricate, and involved: COMPLEX. "We just finished such a S. sugya that we've decided we deserve a break." **2.** Of doubtful validity: QUESTIONABLE. "I heard a S. hezber for that kula, but I'm not convinced it's mutar." **3.** Apparently contradictory: INCONSISTENT. "Rashi here is S. from (because of) Rashi in the Mishna." **4.** Hard to endure: ONEROUS. "During the recession, the matzav was S. for the yeshivos." **5.** Difficult to perform: TOUGH. "It's a S. job to sort all the yeshiva's mail." [<Yid. <HG schwer (heavy, difficult)]

shver-kait (שוועהרקייט) *n., pl.* **shver-kaiten** A perplexing, difficult, or unsolvable question or apparent inconsistency: PROBLEM. "We had a S. figuring out how they made a parve pizza." [cf. shver(e)]

—N.B. The nature of the inconsistency represented by "shverkait" suggests the assumption of a resolution. Compare "stira."

si-man (סימן) *n., pl.* **simunnim 1.** An identifying sign: MARK. "There is a special S. on the bread that is yoshon." **2.** That which signifies evidence or presence of: INDICATION. "The footprints in the snow are a S. that at least some of the bochrim made it across the way to the Beis Medrash." **3.** That which represents evidence or presence of: SYMBOL. "By the Chasidim, some boys wear special clothes as a S. that they are Rebbishe ainiklach." [<Heb. סימן (sign)]

sim-cha (שמחה) *n.* **1.** Festive occasion: CELEBRATION. "The chassuna was a beautiful S." **2.** Great pleasure or enjoyment: DELIGHT. "I had a lot of S. when I heard about your engagement." [<Heb. שמח (rejoice)]

smach (סמך) *n.* Grounds for an opinion: BASIS. "Rebbe brought down a Tosfos as a S. for his pshat in the Taz." [cf. soimech]

so-fek (ספק) *n., pl.* **sfeikos 1.** Unresolved question: UNCERTAINTY. "There's a S. in the Rishoinim about how the Tanna Kama taitshes the posuk." **2.** Doubt in the integrity of: SUSPICION. "The bochrim avoided that restaurant because of a S. in the kashrus." [<Heb. ספק (doubt)]

soif davar (סוף דבר) *Var. of* soif kol soif.

soif kol soif (סוף כל סוף) *interj.* Used to indicate the ultimate result: BOTTOM LINE. "There was a whole shmooze but, S., the Rosh Yeshiva told me to shape up or ship out." [<Heb. סוף (end) + כל (all)] **Var.** soif maise, soif davar.

soif maise (סוף מעשה) *Var. of* soif kol soif.

soi-mech (סומך) *usually followed by "on," p.a.(i)* **1.** To have confidence: RELY. "I'm S. on the Mashgiach when I eat in that restaurant." **2.** To put trust: DEPEND. "At the pool, you have to be S. on the lifeguard to protect you." **3.** To base one's opinion on: ACCREDIT. "He was S. on the Shulchan Aruch for the psak." [<Heb. סמך (lean upon)]

soi-ser (סותר) *p.a.(t)* To imply the opposite or the denial of: GAINSAY, CONTRADICT. "It seems that the Rambam is S. himself, and the Achroinim give what seem to be only doicheke terutzim." [<Heb. סתר (hide, destroy)]

soi-vel (סובל) *p.a.(t)* To manage to tolerate or to deal with: BEAR. "I couldn't be S. the tension, so I made the first step to bury the hatchet." [<Heb. סבל (carry)]

speak out *vt.* **1.** To cite as proof in discourse: ADDUCE. "He S. a few mekoros but had little to say about

them." **2.** To say explicitly: DELINEATE. "The teacher S. the conduct rules so there would be no excuses." [<Eng.]

stam (סתם) *adj. (p.a. only) & adv.* **1.** Usually or commonly expected: ORDINARY. "His expensive new hat is not S." **2.** Easy to solve, learn, do, etc.: ELEMENTARY, ON AN ELEMENTARY LEVEL. "This physics test is not S.; I wish I'd studied more." **3.** Usual or customary: TYPICAL, TYPICALLY. "That bochur is not S.; he learned Kodshim when he was eleven years old." *adv.* **4.** With or for no particular reason: MERELY, JUST, JUST LIKE THAT. "Don't make big theories; I S. decided not to go home for Shabbos." [<Heb. סתם (close)]

sti-ra (סתירה) *n.* A situation in which inherent factors, actions, or propositions are contrary to one another: INCONSISTENCY, OXYMORON. "It's a S. to have a recipe for Sefardi gefilte fish." [cf. soiser]

sug-ya (סוגייא) *n.* A distinct matter for consideration in discussion, thought, or study, particularly in reference to an informal division of the Gemara: TOPIC. "The S. we're learning is too lomdish to say outside." [<Aram. סוג (category)] **Cf.** parsha, inyan.

sva-ra (סברא) *n.* **1.** A reasoning to justify a position: JUSTIFICATION. "I can't find a S. for taking time from learning to play games." **2.** A rational ground or motive: REASON. "I had a S. for shmoozing him out. I want him to be more serious." **3.** Plausible explanation: THEORY. "The S. for a convenience store is that for some items at certain times, people will pay double." [<Heb. סבר (think)]

svi-va (סביבה) *n.* The aggregate of environmental conditions or influences: SURROUNDINGS. "The S. in the yeshiva can occasionally seem cold and impersonal, but no place in the world is more friendly, close, and geshmak." [<Heb. סבב (turn)]

T

tach-lis (תכלית) *n.* **1.** The ultimate result: OUTCOME. "The T. is that we can't get out of our assignment to put away the sforim." **2.** The reason for which something happens: PURPOSE. "The T. for taking the keys now is to get into the kitchen on Motzoei Shabbos to make French fries." **3.** The justification for the existence of something: RAISON D'ETRE. "What's the T. for those valves on the radiators?" [<Heb. כלה (finish)]
—**N.B.** Occasionally used as an interjection with the sense, "Get to the bottom line."

tach-lis-dik(e) (תכלית-דיק) *adj.* Excellent or first-rate: CAPITAL. "His new town car is T." [cf. tachlis]

taf-kid (תפקיד) *n.* A purpose demanding resoluteness and determination: MISSION. "His T. is to bring people closer to Yiddishkait." [<Heb. פקד (appoint)]

tah-ke (טאקע) *adv.* **1.** Really or truly: ACTUALLY, ABSOLUTELY, IN-DEED. "You should T. learn halacha; there's no other way to become a talmid chacham." **2.** In consideration of all the information available: AFTER ALL. "I T. have more in common with the new Chasidishe bochur than I would have thought." *interj.* **3.** Expression of wonderment regarding truth or validity: IS THAT SO? "T.? I never imagined that there could be such major changes in the girsas of Gemaros." [<Yid. <Polish tak (yes)]

tai-nah (טענה) *n.* **1.** A complaint: GRIEVANCE. "I have a T. on you for forgetting to return my sefer." **2.** A say in the matter: OPINION. "So what's your T. on the new carpet in the Beis Medrash." *vi.* **3.** To voice a complaint: GRIPE. "I T. to the Menahel about the lousy food in yeshiva." **4.** To offer an opinion: CLAIM. "I T. we should go vaiter now and ask Rebbe our shaila later." [<Heb. טען (load)]

taitsh (טייטשען) *n.* **1.** The word or words that replace the word or words from another language: TRANSLA-

TION. "Don't ask me all the time; find the T. in a dictionary." **2.** The implicit message of an action or statement: EXPLANATION. "If you're wondering why he's so happy, the T. is he just won $15,000 in the lottery." *vt.* **3.** To render into another language: TRANSLATE. "Try to T. this word by its context." **taitsh up 4.** To evaluate according to accepted prescriptions: INTERPRET, EXPLAIN. "I'm having a hard time trying to T. his odd behavior." [<Yid. <HG Deutsch (German, i.e., indigenous)] —**N.B.** "uptaitsh" is a nominal form for def. 4: INTERPRETATION.

tai-va (תאווה) *n.* **1.** A general desire or inclination for: WEAKNESS. "He has such a T. for ice cream that he never lets himself walk past the freezer section in the market." **2.** The instantiation of a desire or inclination for: CRAVING. "I rarely eat ice cream, so I can't explain why I have such a T. for it lately." **3.** A general or sudden urge: TEMPTATION. "When I see how the yeshiva has to be mechabed that guy just for his money, I have a T. to give him a piece of my mind." **4.** Ardent enthusiasm or zeal: RELISH. "It's great to see that he has such a T. for learning that you can always find him in Beis Medrash." [<Heb. תאו (desire)] **Var.** yetzer hara.

take on *Var. of* nem on [<Eng.]

ta-ko-na (תקנה) *Var. of* gzeira. [<Heb. תקן (fix)]

talk in *vt.* To engage in exchange of ideas about; to articulate intelligent thoughts or opinions about: DISCUSS. "For a guy who never learned in yeshiva, it's impressive how he can T. learning." [<Eng.]

tal-mid cha-cham (תלמיד חכם) *Var. of* chacham, def. 2. [cf. lomdus + cf. chacham]

te-ku-fa (תקופה) *n.* A specified era: PERIOD. "During that T., I had no idea what I wanted to do." [Heb. קיף (encircle)]

tell o-ver *vt.* To recount in an orderly way: RELATE. "No one can T. a maise with every praht the way he can." [<Eng.] **Cf.** say over.

te-rutz (תירוץ) *n., pl.* **terutzim 1.** A spoken or written way to resolve a difficulty or respond to a question about intellectual matters: SOLUTION. "I have such a poshute T. to your kashe that you'll be embarrassed you asked it." **2.** Justification of an action or behavior: EXCUSE. "I have to come up with a T. for getting here so late." *in the phrase* **"to give a terutz" 3.** To pose or present as a possible solution: SUGGEST. "He gave me a T. that the yeshiva changed the curfew to improve safety standards." [<Aram. תרצ (upright)]

te-va (טבע) *n.* **1.** The collective qualities distinctive to and descriptive of a thing or person: CHARACTER. "The

T. of dorm life is that there's never enough of anything but germs." **2.** The physical rules presumed to guide the predictable behavior of the world: NATURE. "It seems to be just T. that the Mashgiach walks in as soon as you pull out the microwave from the back of the closet." [<Heb. טבע (imprint)]

tief (טיעף) *adv.* Deeply and intensely: PROFOUNDLY. "He insulted me T. with that remark of his." [cf. tief(e)]

tief(e) (טיעף) *adj.* Deep and intense: PROFOUND. "His shiur is too T. to let the younger bochrim attend." [<Yid. <HG tief (deep)]

ti-pesh (טפש) *n., pl.* **tipshim** A silly or stupid person: IDIOT. "He felt like a real T. when he failed the simple test and the makeup test." [<Heb. טפש (foolish)]

tip-shus (טפשות) *n.* A silly or stupid act or idea: FOOLERY, MADNESS. "It's T. to walk by the subway late at night." [cf. tipesh]

tip-shus-dik(e) (טפשות-דיק) *adj.* Silly or foolish: RIDICULOUS. "He should be embarrassed to try to publish such a T. sefer." [cf. tipesh]

tir-cha (טירחא) *n.* Cause for undue effort or annoyance: BOTHER. "It's too big a T. to file all these papers; just drop them in a box." [cf. matriach.] —**N.B.** The phrase "a tircha" may be more naturally translated as a p.a.: BOTHERSOME.

tmi-mus-dik(e) (תמימות-דיק) *adj.* Endearingly simple, unaffected, unspoiled, and sincere: NAIVE. "He's too T. to have to be able to deal with shtarke, pruste goyim at work." [<Heb. תם (plain)]

tmi-mus-dike (תמימות-דיקער) *n.* A naive person: INNOCENT. "He's such a T., he can't believe that even some policemen are krum." [cf. tmi-mus-dik(e)]

tnai (תנאי) *n., pl.* **tnoim** A condition or circumstance upon which a certain effect is predicated: STIPULATION. "For my tastes, he has too many T. for giving a ride." [<Aram. תני (second)] —**N.B.** The phrase "al tnai" precedes a conjunction and denotes: ON THE CONDITION, i.e., "You can have a ride al T. that you sit in the back, pay the tolls, don't smoke, and leave your windows up."

to-e-les (תועלת) *n.* **1.** Resultant profit or benefit: GAIN. "There's a big T. in selling cheap snacks near the yeshiva." **2.** A benefit intended for the general good: SERVICE. "There's a big T. in offering more nutritional snacks near the yeshiva." **3.** That which is favorable or desirable to a particular individual: ADVANTAGE. "There's no T. in kissing up to the teacher. He grades straight by the numbers." [<Aram. <Heb. עלה (rise)]

toi-tza-a (תוצאה) The final result of an action: OUTCOME. "His shteler as the head of the Vaad HaRabbonim is the T. of years of learning and some talent with politics." [<Heb. יצא (leave)]

toi-va (טובה) *n.* A kind act: FAVOR. "Do me a T. and get me a Chumash." [<Heb. טוב (good)]

to-leh (תולה) *p.a.(t)* **1.** To cause to depend: HINGE. "We had to be T. our trip on the weather." **2.** To attribute an unsuccessful outcome to: BLAME. "We were T. the cancellation of the trip on the weather." [<Heb. תלה (hang)]

to-lu-i (תלוי) *adj. (p.a. only)* Contingent upon or determined by a condition: DEPENDENT ON. "Our trip is T. on the weather." [cf. toleh] —**N.B.** The p.a. phrase "to be Toleh" can be translated as "to depend upon."

To-rah (תורה) *n.* The entire body of Jewish law and literature based upon, derived from, or associated with the Torah: TORAH. "What is life if not T.?" [<Heb. הרה (teach)]

to-rah (תורה) *n.* The accumulated and organized body of knowledge surrounding a particular subject: SCIENCE. "I guess there's more of a T. in fixing bicycles than I had thought." [cf. Torah] **Var.** shtikl Torah.

to-rud (טרוד) *adj. (p.a. only)* Completely absorbed or involved: PREOCCUPIED. "He was so T. with his learning that he barely realized the

lights had gone off." [<Heb. טרד (involve)]

to-vei-a (תובע) *Var. of* mun.

toy-us (טעות) *n., pl.* **tousim** That which is generally held to be untrue; a mistake: ERROR. "It's a big T. to change your chavrusa so late in the zman." [<Heb. טעה (stray)]

tracht ois (טראכטעז) *vt. & vi.* To think through: CONTEMPLATE. "T. before you make any big decisions." [<Yid. <MHG Tracht (tract)]

tshu-ka (תשוקה) *n.* A deep and sincere desire: LONGING. "I have a T. for ice cream on a hot day like today." [<Heb. שקק (desire)]

tu-mul (טומעל) *n.* **1.** The noisy commotion of a crowd: TUMULT, MELEE. "There was a big T. when those two goyim broke into the Beis Medrash." *vi.* **2.** To be occupied trying to attain something by speaking with others: ARGUE. They T. about why the Rosh Yeshiva wasn't by shachris, but he had just overslept." [<Yid. <HG tummeln (to make noise)]

tu oif (אויפטוהן) *vt.* **1.** To reach an end, especially through some effort: ATTAIN. "He T. a hundred on his physics test." **2.** To get or receive, especially through some effort: OBTAIN. "He T. a second portion from the cook." [<Yid. <HG tun (do, achieve)]

tut zich (זיך-טוהן) *n.* **1.** One who busies himself in order to feel important: HOTSHOT. "The T.'s pants almost fell down while he was running around with those heavy keys and that walkie-talkie." *reflexive verb* **2.** "Before Purim, the bochrim T. to get the best costumes." [<Yid. <HG tun (do, pretend)]

tvi-a (תביעה) *n.* Cause of dissatisfaction: GRIEVANCE. "My chavrusa had a T. on me for coming late." [<Heb. תבע (claim)]

two dots *n.* *(pl.)* An indication that a particular portion of the gemara is finished: COLON. "If you want to follow shiur, learn at least up to the T." [<Eng.]

tzad (צד) *n., pl.* **tzdud-dim 1.** The reasoning behind one side of a doubt or dilemma: BASIS. "What's your T. to switch yeshivos?" **2.** One possibility within a question, argument, or doubt: SIDE. "It seems poshut; I can't hear the two T. in this inyan." **3.** The assumption of truth, especially for the sake of argument: SUPPOSITION. "On the T. that you're also going, I can give you a ride." [<Heb. צד (side)]

tzad ha-sha-veh (צד השווה) A shared trait or theme: COMMON DENOMINATOR. "The T. between a bus and a pencil is that they're both yellow." [cf. tzad + <Heb. שוה (even)]

tzo-rich i-yun (צריך עיון) *n.* **1.** Someone or something displaying that which deviates from the norm: ENIGMA. "The guy who was laughing throughout the musar shmooze is a T." *adj.* *(p.a. only)* **"a tzorich iyun" 2. a.** Being without resolution: UNANSWERED. "Many questions in science remain a T. even today." **b.** Not easily understood: UNCLEAR. "Unless you can change the girsa, the whole sugya's a T." **c.** In a state of unresolved puzzlement: PERPLEXED. "The achroinim try a few terutzim, but most blaib a T." [<Heb. צרך (need) + עין (eye)]

tzu-bro-chen(e) (צובראכען) *adj.* **1.** Weakened in spirit: BROKENHEARTED. "He was really T. when he lost his money." **2.** Sad or depressed by the failure of hopes or expectations: DISAPPOINTED. "He was T. because he failed his driving test." [<Yid. <HG zubrochen (broken)]

tzu-floi-gen(e) (צופלויגען) *adj.* **1.** Bewildered and unable to be aware of goings on: DAZED. "He awoke lying on the ground, looking T. and moaning in agony." **2.** Sloppy and in a state of disarray: UNKEMPT. "After two hours of tennis, he stood drinking a soda and looking totally T." **3.** Capricious, disorganized, and irresponsible: FLIGHTY. "He's so T., I'm surprised he remembers to get dressed every morning." [<Yid. <HG fliegen (fly)]

tzu-fried-en(e) (צופריעדען) *adj.* Complacent with, resigned to, or satisfied with a circumstance: CONTENT. "I did my best, so I guess I'm T. with my grade." [<Yid. <HG zufrieden (satisfied)]

tzu-fried-en-kait (צופריעדען-קייט) *n.* Complacency or satisfaction: CONTENTMENT. "Since I got married, I've reached a real T. with my life." [cf. tzufrieden(e)]

tzum ersht-ins *Var. of* ershtins.

tzu-shtel (צושטעלען) *n.* **1.** Estimation of a composite likeness: COMPARISON. "Rebbe made a T. from a Mishna in Kodshim." **2.** A kind or point of likeness: SIMILARITY. "There's a T. between our sugya and the Mishna in Kodshim." [cf. shtel tzu]

U-V-W

u-ge-ret (אונגערעהדט) *adj. (p.a. only)* Easily seen or understood: EVIDENT, OBVIOUS. "It's U. from nature that Hashem created the world." [<Yid. <HG ohne (without) + reden (talk)]

un-ge-zetzt(e) (אונגעזעצט) *adj.* Uncharacteristically gloomy or melancholy: DEPRESSED. "Some bochrim become U. when they feel their learning is shvach." [<Yid. <HG setzen (set)]

un-ze-re (אונזערע) *adj.* Related to and presuming a group with which the speaker is associated: OUR(S). "The fraie family in the neighborhood is not from U. oilam." [<Yid. <HG unser (our)]

up-shlug (אפשלאגען) *n.* Proof that an assertion is false and that any claim based upon it is ineffective: REFUTATION. "You do realize that your pshat would be an U. to Rebbe's chidush, don't you?" [cf. shlug up.]

up-taitsh (אפטייטש) **Cf.** taitsh up.

va-da (וודאי) *adv.* **1.** With certainty: UNDOUBTEDLY. "I'll V. go to seder, even if it snows." *n.* **2.** Circumstance about which there is no doubt: CERTAINTY. "The end of the sale is a V.; you should chap arain now." [<Aram. <Heb. ודה (admit)] **Var.** avada.

vaist ois (אויס-ווייזען) *adv.* Outwardly apparent or evident: OSTENSIBLY. "V. the appeal was a success; the yeshiva hasn't sent anyone collecting by the balebatim." [<Yid. <HG Weise (manner) + cf. ois]

vait (ווייט) *adv.* Being more involved in a subject than is necessary or desired: DEEPLY. "He didn't want to go too V. into the zaitike sugya, since Tosfos only brought it down as a raya to be mechazek his ikar chidush." [cf. vait(e)]

vait(e) (ווייט) *adj.* **1.** Away from that which is correct or good: ASTRAY, DISTANT. "It was sad to see how the ungezetzte bochur began to grow V. from Yiddishkait." **2.** Strained and improbable: FARFETCHED. "The terutz was so V. that Rebbe was barely goires it." [<Yid. <HG weit (far)]

vait-er (װײטער) *adj.* **1.** More distant: FARTHER. "Maybe we should get off at the next exit; go V. and ask someone." **2.** At a more advanced point: FURTHER. "Your kashe shows up V. in Tosfos, on amud beiz." [cf. vait(e)]

vaks ois (אויסװאקסען) *vi.* **1.** To realize potential: DEVELOP. "I want my son to V. into a talmid chacham." **2.** To attain full development: MATURE. "It's gratifying to watch the wild, young bochrim V. and settle down." [<Yid. <HG wachsen (grow)]

varf (װארפען) *vt.* To bring to public attention, as to show off: FLAUNT, BRANDISH. "He was convinced everyone was impressed when he V. the little bit of lomdus he remembered from yeshiva." [<Yid. <HG warfen (throw)]

ve-ha-ra-ya (והא ראיה) *conj.* Evidenced by the fact that: CONSEQUENTLY, AND TO PROVE IT. "The dorm is overcrowded, V. one of my roommates has to sleep with his feet in the closet." [cf. raya] **Cf.** haraya.

velt (װעלט) *n.* **1.** A particular class of people with common interests, aims, etc.: COMMUNITY. "The yeshiva V. frowns on going to college." **2.** A great number of people or things: MULTI-TUDE. "A V. of people came to the Siyum HaShas at Madison Square Garden." **3.** A great deal: WEALTH, TON. "There's a V. of reading to do before I'm ready for the test." *pronoun* **the velt 4.** All or each of a particular class: EVERYONE. "The V. decided to chip in for one chassuna present." [<Yid. <HG Welt (world)]

vep (װעפען) *n.* One who is uninteresting and who lacks animation: BORE. "I was stuck next to some V. for four hours in the plane. I couldn't bear talking to him." [<Yid. <MFr vapeur (vapid)] **Var.** vepper.

vep-per (װעפער) *Var. of* vep.

vep-pish(e) (װעפען) *Var. of* veppy.

vep-py (װעפען) *adj.* **1.** Tedious; lacking spirit: VAPID. "For me, my conversation with the old lady was V., but I think it made her happy to have someone to talk to." **2.** Unappealing to prevalent tastes or trends: LAME. "The movies they let you watch in camp are so V., you don't want to watch them anyway." [cf. vep] **Var.** veppish(e).

ve-ze-hu (וזהו) *interj.* And no more: AND THAT'S IT. "Stop asking for money; I'll give ten more dollars V." [<Heb. (esp. Israeli)זה (this) + הוא (it)]

vi-bahlt (וויא-באלד) *conj.* Inasmuch as: SINCE. "V. I like science, I went to the museum." [<Yid. <HG wie (how) + cf. bahlt]

vild(e) (װילד) *adj.* **1.** Bizarre in theory or conception: FANTASTIC. "He never agrees with Rebbe because he has these V. ideas about learning." **2.** Reckless and fearless: DAUNTLESS. "He has his V. chevra take the subway at all hours." **3.** Relentless and pitiless: FEROCIOUS. "The V. bochur was uncontrollable when he got angry." **4.** Disorganized, flighty, and capricious: CHAOTIC. "The meeting was too V. to accomplish anything of value." [<Yid. <HG wild (wild)]

vort (װארט) *n., pl.* **verter 1.** Any material that imparts beneficial knowledge: LESSON. "I heard a good V. that you can use in your appeal." **2.** A concisely expressed precept: MORAL. "I heard the whole maise, but I didn't chap the V." [<Yid. <HG Wort (word)]

wash *vi. In the phrase* **"make a wash"** In yeshiva, a sporadic, cursory attempt to avoid comments from one's parents and peers: DO ONE'S LAUNDRY. "I'd better make a W. before I can't find the floor." [<Eng.]

what's pshat *Interrogative conj.* Introducing a request for an underlying reason or cause: HOW COME, WHY. "W. the yeshiva gives an entrance exam if they seem to accept everyone who applies?" [<Eng. + cf. pshat]

Y

yash-rus (ישרות) *n.* **1.** Moral upright-ness: JUSTICE. "Your scheme will work, but I question its Y." **2.** Appro-priate thoughtfulness: CONSIDER-ATION. "If you're not going to the chassuna, you should R.S.V.P. as a matter of Y." *adj. (p.a. only)* **3.** *Var. of* yashrusdik(e) [<Heb. ישר (straight)]

yash-rus-dik(e) (ישרות-דיק) *adj.* Free from bias or self-interest: FAIR. "Hagam it worked out against me, I hold the Beiz Din's decision is Y." [cf. yashrus] **Var. (as p.a. only)** yashrus.

ye-di-os (ידיעות) *n.* **1.** That which serves as the basis of educated opin-ions: INFORMATION. "I have no Y. on where most of my old chavrusas are today." **2.** Understanding of the fun-damental and essential elements of some area of study: KNOWLEDGE, KEN. "I have no Y. about dikduk, so go ask someone else." [<Heb. ידע (know)]

ye-shi-va (ישיבה) *n.* A school devoted to Torah study: ACADEMY. "Even after I leave, I always plan to have a shaichus with the yeshiva." [<Heb. ישב (sit)]

ye-shi-vish(e) (ישיביש) *adj.* **1.** Marked by the norms of tastes, style, or man-ner typical of yeshivas: CONSERVA-TIVE. "I don't think that wild tie is Y. enough for where you plan to learn next zman." **2.** Not conforming to ac-cepted standards of etiquette: INDE-COROUS. "He looks really Y. with his creased shirt sticking out even more than his Brisker payos." **3.** Of inferior or obsolete quality or worth: CHEAP. "The fact that no two doors are the same color make the car all the more Y." **4.** Employing or displaying predetermined or universally accepted (and perhaps unoriginal) characteris-tics: TYPICAL, HACKNEYED. "The shiur started with some gevaltike, shvere kashes, but gave just the usual Y. terutzim." **5.** Holding fast to the views common to yeshivas: ADHER-ENT. "He has a good head, but he's too Y. to think for himself." **6.** Giving hanaa to aza sort of bochrim who

105

mamash hold of all the reid, shprach, maises, and general shtik that shaf the mahus of the yeshiva velt: GESH-MAK(E). "You have to live Y. to know Y." [cf. yeshiva]

ye-soid (יסוד) *n., pl.* **yesoidos** Basis, or essential, guiding principle: FUNDA-MENTAL. "The Y. of this store is to sell anything, as long as it costs under $1.00." [<Heb. יסד (foundation)] —**N.B.** "yesoid hadavar," as a variant form, refers to the basis of a previously determined notion.

ye-soid ha-da-var (יסוד הדבר) **Cf.** yesoid.

ye-tzer ha-ra (יצר הרע) *Var. of* taiva.

yi-yush (יאוש) *n.* Sense of giving up hope: DESPAIR. "There was a general feeling of Y. once the bochrim found out about the yeshiva's financial troubles." [cf. meyayesh]

yoi-tzeh (יוצא) *p.a.(t & i)* **1.** To perform or fulfill the requirements of: EXECUTE. "Just call your grand-mother and like that you can be Y. what your mother asked you to do." **2.** To avoid the active fulfillment of a requirement by allowing another to serve as one's surrogate: DIS-CHARGE. "I can't force myself to drink wine now; I'll be Y. kiddush with you." *p.a.(i)* **3.** To perform only that which one is minimally charged to do: DO ONE'S DUTY. "I don't like the idea of going to English, but I'll go just to be Y." **4.** To do just enough to pass muster: GET BY. "I can't take the time to write a good paper for English; I'll write something just to be Y." [<Heb. יצא (exit)]

yu-chid (יחיד) *n., pl.* **yechidim** A distinct entity, particularly a person: IN-DIVIDUAL. "The yeshiva sent an appeal card to every Y., even a separate one for a husband and a wife." [<Heb. יחד (together)] —**N.B.** may connote a "lone wolf," someone acting alone, i.e., "You can't blame everyone for the acts of a Y." or "He was a Y. in his support for the unpopular decision."

Z

zach (זאך) *n., pl.* **zachen 1.** A material object; affairs; actions; thoughts; or belongings: THING. "This Z. isn't bad, but the other Z. is useful for more Z." **2.** Salient feature: POINT. "I want to help him, but the Z. is that he needs to learn to take care of himself." [<Yid. <HG sach (thing)]

zai ge-bensht (זיי געבענטשט) *interj.* Phrase indicating no expectation of any favorable outcome from a conversation or joint venture: YOU'RE HOPELESS. "The speeder passed the others and called out, 'Z.'" [<Yid. <HG sein (be) + <Fr. benir (bless)]

zai ge-zunt (זיי געזונט) *interj.* A recommendation for greater sophistication or awareness: GET REAL. "You think you have a system for winning the lottery? Z!" [<Yid. <HG sein (be) + cf. gezunt(e)]

zait-ik(e) (זייטיק) *adj.* Marginally or subordinately related or associated: TANGENTIAL, PERIPHERAL. "That's an interesting shaila, but it's Z., and we'll save it for another time." [<Yid. <HG Seite (side)]

za-riz (זריז) *n.* A reliable and complaisant person: STALWART. "He's a real Z.; you can count on him." [cf. zrizus]

zchus (זכות) *n., pl.* **zchusim 1.** Quality of reward, merit, or commendation: VIRTUE. "I hold that his yashrus is his biggest Z." **2.** An advantage or honor considered to be a reward: PRIVILEGE. "I hold it to be a Z., not a tircha, to look after my grandparents." **3.** That which one is entitled to: RIGHT. "You have no Z. to use my things without asking me for reshus." **4.** Acknowledgment for a worthy quality or act: RECOGNITION. "In the Z. of this donation, may you earn enough to give more next year." [cf. zoiche]

zei-yar (זייער) *adv.* To a very high degree: EXTREMELY. "The food around here is Z. bad." [<Yid. <HG sehr (very)]

107

zel-ba(זעלבע) *adj.* Being as that which has been mentioned or is known: USUAL, SAME. "However they cook it, it's the Z. cut-rate meat." [<Yid. <HG selbst (self)]

zetz ain (איינזעצען) *vt.* To offer a plausible explanation for: RATIONAL-IZE. "The gemara Z. the mishna to say it's talking about a heicha timtza of borrowed money." [<Yid. <HG setzen (set)]

zich-er (זיכער) *adj.* *(p.a. only)* **1.** Sure or determined: CERTAIN. "I'm Z. that I left it here, but now I can't find it." *adv.* **2.** Without doubt: DEFINITELY. "I'm Z. leaving in an hour, so hurry up if you want to come with me." [<Yid. <HG sicher (sure)]

zman (זמן) *n., pl.* **zmanim 1.** A division or portion of a specified duration: TIME. "There's a Z. for sleeping, but it's not during shiur." **2.** Any of the semesters into which a yeshiva's academic year is divided: TERM. "The learning is shtark in Elul Z. but a shtikl shvach in summer Z." [<Heb. זמן (time)]

zoi-che (זוכה) *p.a.(i)* Granted special advantage (usually as a Divine reward): PRIVILEGED, MANAGE. "I hope I'm Z. to stay in learning for many more years." [<Heb. זכה (warrant)]

zri-zus (זריזות) *n.* **1.** Enthusiasm and cheer about performing a specific act or job: ALACRITY. "It's a pleasure to see how the bochrim come to learn with such Z." **2.** Dependability for proper and efficient accomplishment: RELIABILITY. "Rebbe put him in charge since he has a lot of Z." [<Heb. זרז (urge)]

zuhg (זאגען) *n.* A clever remark: LINE. "I heard a good Z. about a guy who tried to define the Yeshivish language and could only make a haschala." [<Yid. <HG sagen (say)]

About the Author

Chaim Weiser teaches high-school English in a major American yeshiva. He is a specialist in translation and has written several articles on the challenges of translation and on educational theory. Weiser is the author of *A Silent, Invisible Language: An Exploration of Written English* and is a consultant to the Translation Division of Abell Communication of Antwerp, Belgium. He received his education in yeshivas in America and abroad and holds degrees in education and linguistics from American University in Washington, DC. He lives with his wife, Tamar, within listening distance of the yeshiva where he teaches.